BIBLE ETHICS

by

John and Sara Miles

Illustrator: Alice Foster

---

*Developed in Cooperation With
the ICI International Office Staff*

International Correspondence Institute
Chaussée de Waterloo, 45
1640 Rhode-Saint-Genèse
(Brussels) Belgium

Address of the ICI office in your area:

Scripture quotations are from the New International Version (NIV) and Good New Bible (Today's English Version)
© American Bible Society, 1976. Used by permission. The King James's Version (KJV) is also quoted.

To be used with: Student Report 1991 Edition

First Edition 1979
Second Edition 1980
   Reprinted 1981
   Reprinted 1984
Third Edition 1991

© 1979, 1980, 1991
All Rights Reserved
International Correspondence Institute
Irving, Texas, USA
6/91 5M BA

L6160E92   ISBN 1-56390-009-2

Contents

	Page
First, Let's Have a Talk	5

Lesson

1	God Made You What You Are	8
2	God is the Pattern for Our Lives	28
3	What God Wants You to Be and Do	42
4	God Gives You Rules for Living	58
5	God Gives You Standards for Living	78
6	God Wants You to Care for Yourself	100
7	God Wants You to Care for the Church	124
8	God Sent You to Care for the World	140

First, Let's Have a Talk

From Your Study Guide Author

Far too often we think about the things we cannot do because we are Christians. But, the purpose of right living should be as Jesus said, "Be holy because I am holy" (1 Peter 1:16).

The idea of positive living means to show the right actions in your life-style as a Christian following the example found in the life and teaching of Jesus: positive commands and promises rather than just demands brings fulfillment and joyful living instead of frustration.

Jesus is our example. We are personally responsible for cooperating with Christ to bring about positive living which results from our love for Him.

This course will help you see the rules which were made to help you be holy as He is holy. It will help you see that these rules for right living are made for your own good. God is interested in what you *are* rather than in what you don't do as a Christian.

Your Study Guide

Bible Ethics is a pocket-sized workbook that you can take with you and study whenever you have some free time. Try to set aside some time every day to study it.

Be sure to study carefully the first two pages of each lesson. This prepares your mind for what follows. Next, study the lesson, section by section and follow the instructions under the title *For You To Do*. If there is not room to write your answers in the study guide, write them in a notebook so you can refer back to them when you review the lesson. If you are studying this course with a group, follow the instructions of your group leader.

You will notice that *objectives* are given at the beginning of each lesson. The word *objective* is used in this book to help you know what to expect from your study. An *objective* is something like a goal, or a purpose. You will study better if you keep in mind your *objectives*.

Your Student Report

If you are studying to earn a certificate; you have received a separate booklet called *Student Report: Bible Ethics*. Fill out the student report when told to do so in Lessons 4 and 8.

Follow the instructions given in your student report for sending it to the ICI office in your area. The address should be stamped on the second page of this study guide, or on the back of the student report. If it is

First, Let's Have a Talk

not there, send the report to the ICI Brussels address given on the back of the student report. When you do this, you will receive an attractive certificate, or a seal, if you have already earned the certificate by completing another course in this unit of courses.

About the Authors

John and Sara Miles are a husband-and-wife team who have drawn from their rich background in missionary and teaching experience to give us this course. John Miles, whose Ph.D. is in the French language, is presently director of the department of French at Wheaton College, Wheaton, Illinois, U.S.A. Sara Miles, who holds master of religious education and master of science (biology) degrees, is presently a biology instructor and career counselor at Wheaton College. They served as missionary teachers in Zaire, Africa, from 1965 to 1968. Both are ordained ministers.

Now you are ready to study Lesson 1. God bless you as you study!

Lesson 1

God Made You What You Are

Knowing that you are somebody is important. It helps you *feel* good inside. It also helps you *do* things.

The Bible tells us about a man named Gideon who thought he was not important. He was hiding from the enemy that had invaded his country. When Gideon had given up all hope for this people, God sent an angel to encourage him. The angel had this message: "The Lord is with you, brave and mighty man."

God did not look at Gideon to see what he had done to be important. Instead, God saw what could be done with His help. God helped Gideon lead this people. (Read Judges 6-8.) - Do THIS TOMORROW!

Think of Gideon and take courage. You may not *feel* important, but you *are—in God's eyes*. Because you are somebody to Him, He wants you to feel and act that way. People soon knew that the Lord was with Gideon. He behaved differently. That's what God wants you to do too. He wants you to behave differently because He is with you, and you are somebody!

In this lesson you will study...

You Are Somebody: A Child of God
   God Has Done a Work in You
   Purpose for You as His Child
You Are Somebody: A Member of Christ's Body
   God Has Placed You in a Family
   Purpose for You in the Family
You Are Somebody: An Ambassador of the Kingdom
   God Has Left You in the World
   Purpose for You in the World

This lesson will help you...

- Explain in a sentence or two how important you are as a child of God and how this has an effect on your life.

- Describe your personal responsibility for living as God's child according to God's Word.

YOU ARE SOMEBODY: A CHILD OF GOD

Objective 1. *Explain what happened to you when you became a Christian.*

What happened to you when you became a Christian? So many things! And the Bible talks about them in many ways! You repented of your sin, and God forgave you. You were saved because you asked Jesus Christ to become your Savior. At the same time you took Jesus as Lord of your life. You *believed* in Him as the Son of God and *received* Him into your heart, to rule over your life.

God Has Done a Work in You

The Gospel of John tells us what a wonderful thing takes place when people receive Jesus Christ as Lord and Savior. Read these verses carefully:

> Some, however, did receive him and believed in him; so he gave them the right to become God's children. They did not become God's children by natural means, that is, by being born as the children of a human father; God himself was their Father (John 1:12-13).

Was this only for those who lived at the time of Jesus? No, of course not. To be born again is the right and experience of all who have ever believed and received Jesus. We are made new through the Holy Spirit.

In a special way God has given life to you. It is not a

God Made You What You Are

new *physical* life—no one can go back to being a baby. It is a new *spiritual* life, which God Himself brings into being. He is the Father of all who are born again. We are His children.

So, if you are a Christian believer, you are a child of God. Can you imagine how important that makes you? You really are somebody! *You* are a child of the Almighty God. The Creator of the universe is *your* Father.

For You to Do

In each of these *For You to Do* sections, the questions or exercises will help you review or apply what you have just studied. Answer the questions if space is given, or follow the special directions. For long answers, write the answer in a notebook and use the notebook whenever you want to make notes about the lesson.

For these two exercises, choose the best answer to each question. Circle the letter in front of your choice.

1 What two things does John 1:12 tell us we need to do to become God's children?
  a) Forgive and forget others
  ⓑ Receive and believe Jesus
  c) Become a baby and grow again

2 When you became a Christian, what work did God do in you?
  a) He made you His child and helped you want to behave in a better way.
  b) He made you feel more important than other people.

Check your answers at the end of this lesson.

Purpose for You as His Child

Objective 2. *List the three areas in your personal life for which God has a purpose.*

When you read that God is your Heavenly Father, perhaps you think of your own father. What was your father like when you were a child? Certainly, he was not perfect as God is perfect. A good father loves his children. He wants them to have the best he can provide. He wants them to have a happy and complete life, and be the best they can be.

God, our Heavenly Father, wants the same for us. He wants the best for His children. He has a purpose for our new lives as Christians. God wants us to be happy as we fulfill His purpose for our lives.

In Ephesians 2, we learn about what great things God has done for us. We *were* like everyone else—spiritually dead, following our own desires. But God has made us alive in Jesus Christ. This new life is the gift of God received by faith in Jesus. We read these words about what it means to become a child of God:

God has made us what we are, and in our union with Christ Jesus he has created us for a life of good deeds, which he has already prepared for us to do (Ephesians 2:10).

The purpose of God for His children is "a life of good deeds." "Good deeds" mean doing what is good and right in all things. We should use all our time and talents to be the best we can become. This is what will make our Heavenly Father happy. Doing good deeds for our Father is what will give us a happy and complete life!

Remember that good deeds can not make anyone a Christian. In Ephesians 2:8-9, we learn that salvation is not earned. It is a gift of God. But once a person has become a child of God, he lives according to what he believes. A child of God is different and acts differently from people who are not Christians. He shows his faith in his new life by doing new things for God. This is the message we find in James 1:22-26—faith has to show itself in action.

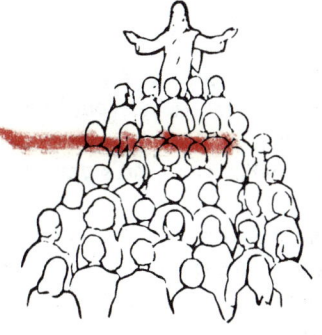

For You to Do

Circle the letter that best completes each sentence below.

3 God's purpose for your life as a believer is to have you (GOOD DEEDS)
a) earn your salvation.
b) do good and right in all things.

4 James 1:22-26 tells us not only to listen to God's Words but to
a) read them often.
b) wonder what they mean.
c) put them into practice.

Check your answers.

We have talked about God's purpose for the Christian in terms of good deeds. It is important for you to understand, however, that what you do is an outward sign of what you *are*. You *are* somebody—you *are* God's child! But what will God's child be like?

> Even before the world was made, God had already chosen us to be his through our union with Christ, so that we would be holy and without fault before him (Ephesians 1:4).

God Made You What You Are 15

God wants His children to become holy and without fault. You know that the believer *is* a new creation, he *is* reborn. You can also know from your Bible reading and from experience that a Christian *is not* instantly perfect. Even the disciples had faults. But God wants all His children to *become* holy and good. That takes time; like a child growing up. In fact, our growth will not be complete until we are in heaven.

GOD'S CHILD

Is	→ A new creation
Is not	→ Instantly perfect
Is to become	→ Holy and faultless

↑↑ READ CAREFULLY ↑↑↑

A carpenter may hope that his son will be a skillful carpenter. A singer may want his daughter to become a great musician. But does being born into a certain family give a child the skill of his father? No. It takes time, teaching, and practice to develop any skill. The child has to want to learn from his father. He also has to try to do what his father wants to teach him.

Every believer is born again according to the will of God. His heart is changed and he has a new life. That is God's purpose for the believer. Then God wants him to live a life of good deeds. The only way the believer can do this is to let God help him change his *attitudes*. *Attitudes* are the ways we feel about people and things.

Our attitude will show what we are like, just as our faces sometimes do. This picture shows us how God changes us.

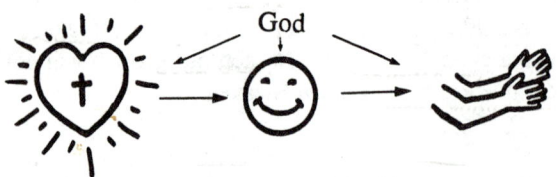

1 New Life   2 New Attitudes   3 New Actions

First, God saves us and changes our inner life. Then our new life produces new attitudes which He wants to make holy and faultless. These new attitudes lead us to new actions. Do you see that the new life, the new feelings, and the good deeds are all part of God's purpose? That is one definition of Bible ethics: putting your new life into practice in your attitude and your actions. Do you also see that in each area the believer has to be willing to receive God's help?

For You to Do

5 Make a list in your notebook of the things about which God has changed your feelings and your actions. Are you encouraged by what God has done in your life?

God Made You What You Are 17

6 Match the words which indicate God's purpose for your life (right column) with the three areas of your life they affect (left column). Write the number on the blank provided.

.3.. **a** Actions 1) Be saved
..1. **b** New life 2) Be holy and faultless
.2.. **c** Attitudes 3) Do good

Check your answers..

YOU ARE SOMEBODY: A MEMBER OF CHRIST'S BODY

Objective 3. *Explain why God has placed you in the body of Christ.*

You may have heard someone say something like this: "If you were the only sinner in the world, Jesus would have died for you!" But you weren't the only one, were you? It was part of God's plan of salvation that *many* should be saved. You were included, of course. The suffering of Jesus was "in order to bring many *sons* to share his glory" (Hebrews 2:10). God intended his Son, Jesus, to be "the first among *many* brothers" (Romans 8:29).

Do you think the words "sons" and "brothers" do not include you if you are a woman? No, you have an equal right to be called a "son of God." Remember: those who believed and received had the right to become God's children!

God Has Placed You in a Family

God has many sons and daughters: the Christians who form the family of God. Our Father wants His family to be a united group. The Bible expresses this by calling God's family "the body of Christ."

A body is a unit formed of many parts all working for one purpose. How different the parts are! But how much they need each other! Christ's body is like that. It is formed of Christians from different countries, races, and ages. Yet it is unified—made into one body, and one family.

> So then, you Gentiles are not foreigners or strangers any longer; you are now fellow-citizens with God's people and members of the family of God (Ephesians 2:19).

Unity is wonderful! It is good for you to recognize that we are made one with other believers. But God didn't make Christians one body just to have a unit. A soccer coach does not collect players just to say that he has a team. He unifies them to play! God has a purpose for the body of Christ, and you have a part to play in it.

Purpose for You in the Family

Why did God place people in families? Think of an orphan or a widow in your town. It is easy to see that people *need* people. The family is God's way of meeting needs, both physical and emotional. Together a family can provide the food and housing needed by the members. Together it can meet the need of each person for love and respect.

God placed each of His children in His family for the same reason—because we need each other. Perhaps you do not feel the need for other Christians to help you with your physical or emotional needs. Perhaps you have a family in which you are loved and cared for. But your brothers in Christ may need your help in these ways. Without a doubt, you have an important part in the ministry to these other members of the family.

What is clear is that we all need to take part in the spiritual life of God's family. The writer to the Hebrews puts the physical, emotional, and spiritual needs together.

> Let us be concerned for one another, to help one another to show love and to do good. Let us not give up the habit of meeting together, as some are doing. Instead, let us encourage one another all the more, since you see that the Day of the Lord is coming nearer (Hebrews 10:24-25).

By meeting with your Christian brothers, you can meet needs and have needs met. This is where ethics come in. You can put this new life into practice by helping the family of God. Paul gives us an example of his attitude and deeds when he says:

> Surely you have heard that God in his grace has given me this work to do for your good (Ephesians 3:2).

God wants us to live for the good of others in the body of Christ.

For You to Do

7 Circle the letter before each TRUE statement about God and His family.

T — **a** God wants His children to minister to each other.
F — **b** All men are God's children. Women are too
T — **c** We should not despise other Christians: God has made them our brothers, too.
T — **d** Christ's body exists to meet members' needs.

8 Think about the Christian brothers in your community. What needs do they have? Are you part of God's answer to those needs?

YOU ARE SOMEBODY: AN AMBASSADOR OF THE KINGDOM

Objective 4. *Give an example of your responsibility as a believer to the world.*

God Made You What You Are 21

What would happen to a family which did not grow? Families are meant to increase in number, aren't they? When God created the first human beings, He told them what to do (Genesis 1:28). God wanted Adam and Eve to have children. God wants the same for His family. He wants more and more people to be born again into His family. Do you remember Jesus' words about this?

> Go then to all peoples everywhere and make them my disciples (Matthew 28:19).

Christ's body of believers has to grow, and each member has a share in this process. You are commanded to help by doing your best to bring more believers into God's family.

God Has Left You in the World

This lesson began by asking what happened when you became a Christian. One thing did *not* happen. You did *not* suddenly leave this world and go to heaven. Yet being with the Lord in heaven is far better than life here on earth (Philippians 1:23). God could have taken you to be with Him, but He chose not to.

Probably another thing did *not* happen when you became a child of God. All the problems of money and work did not suddenly disappear. Your neighbors and fellow-workers did not suddenly become more friendly and helpful. Why not? You were still left in this world. And here, things are not always easy. Problems are mixed with joys. You may have harder decisions to make than before you were a Christian. Things may have become more difficult because you have become a Christian. First, your family and friends may not understand you. And second, the devil (who is an evil angel opposed to all God's good work) is against you now.

But look at Jesus' prayer to God for His disciples:

> I do not ask you to take them out of the world, but I do ask you to keep them safe from the Evil One. Just as I do not belong to the world, they do not belong to the world. . . . I sent them into the world, just as you sent me into the world (John 17:15-16, 18).

If God wants His children in the world, you can be sure that there is a good reason.

For You to Do

Choose the correct answer from those given and write them on the space provided.

9 As a believer, we have a responsibility to ..tell..
(tell/argue with)
all people everywhere about God's family
(Adam and Eve/God's family)

Purpose for You in the World

Objective 5. *Describe God's purpose for you in the world as an ambassador for Christ.*

God Made You What You Are 23

Some Christians would like to separate themselves from other people. They leave their homes, families, and villages to live away from the world. That is not what God intended. His plan for you, and for all His children, is for you to do His work in the world. Jesus told His disciples: "As the Father sent me, so send I you" (John 20:21). You are sent to the world just as much as Peter, James, and John, Jesus' disciples. You are to represent the Lord to those around you.

Listen to what Paul says about Christians living as God's representatives:

> Do everything without complaining or arguing, so that you may be innocent and pure as God's perfect children, who live in a world of corrupt and sinful people. You must shine among them like stars lighting up the sky, as you offer them the message of life (Philippians 2:14-16).

You see that your job involves *being*, *feeling*, and *doing*. You are to be God's child, innocent and pure. You are to feel like God's child, happy and obedient, not grumbling. You are to act as His child, doing everything you can for others and telling them about Christ.

A person who represents his or her country in a foreign land is called an ambassador. He is important. Others recognize what he is and where he comes from. In that foreign land, he speaks with authority when his own country's interests are involved.

You are an ambassador. You represent the Kingdom of God in the world. The apostle Paul expresses this very idea in 2 Corinthians 5:20. In the King James Version of the Bible, we read: "We are ambassadors for Christ." Now let's read the whole verse in Today's English Version:

> Here we are, then, speaking for Christ, as though God himself were making his appeal through us (2 Corinthians 5:20).

God's purpose for you in the world is for you to speak for Christ. You represent Him and His heavenly kingdom. God sends you to show and tell people that God loves them and wants to give them new life. What privilege could be greater? What responsibility could be more challenging? What activity places a greater demand on you in terms of putting your new life into practice through your attitudes and actions?

God's purpose for you is a high one. No man by his own power could fulfill it. But you are born again by the Spirit of God, and He lives in you to help you do what you couldn't do before. The Holy Spirit helps you live out your new nature in attitudes and actions worthy of a child of God. But you have to let Him help you, by doing what He tells you to do. You are responsible yourself for the way you live out what God has entrusted to you. Paul's encouragement to Timothy is a good reminder that you must make an effort.

> Do your best to win full approval in God's sight as a worker who is not ashamed of his work (2 Timothy 2:15).

God your Father is eager to help you become a child who is doing his best to grow up to be and feel and act

God Made You What You Are

like Him. He wants you to learn what it is to have a Bible-based way of life, a Christian ethic.

For You to Do

10 Write Philippians 2:14-16 in your notebook. Then, underline the words that can help you live a better life. Study this passage until you know it.

11 As an ambassador for Christ who do you represent?
Christ on earth

12 Circle the letter before each TRUE statement below.

F **a** As a believer you are to complain about others who are not living right.

T **b** God's purpose for you in the world is to be His light and speak for Him.

T **c** You are responsible for the way you live your new life as a child of God.

Check Your Answers

The answers to your study exercises are not given in the usual order. They have been mixed up so that you will not see the answer to your next question ahead of time. Try not to look ahead.

7 a True.
  b False.
  c True.
  d True.

1 b) Receive and believe Jesus.

8 Your answer.

2 a) He made you His child and helped you want to behave in a better way.

9 tell
God's family.

3 b) do good and right in all things.

10 Your answer.

4 c) put them into practice.

11 Christ here on earth.

5 Your answer.

12 a False.   **6 a** 3) Do good.
  b True.   **b** 1) Be saved.
  c True.   **c** 2) Be holy and faultless.

Lesson 2: God is the Pattern For Our Lives

Many countries have a saying such as "like father, like son." An interesting thing about families is the likenesses between members. For example, we have two children—a girl and a boy. Both have big brown eyes like their father. The boy has curly hair like his father; the girl has straight hair like her mother. People usually say that they look alike, and "just like their dad."

Of course, family likenesses can be seen in our attitudes and actions too. We were upset with our little boy just this morning because, instead of dressing, he was reading! Then we remembered how many times our parents were angry with both of us for that same love for books. We also loved to read and did not always choose the right times.

There is also a family likeness that is spiritual. Jesus told the Pharisees, who thought they were so good but were not: "You are the children of your father, the Devil, and you want to follow your father's desires" (John 8:44). If Christians are indeed God's children, they will show a family likeness in their nature, attitudes, and actions.

Just as a child watches his earthly father and copies what he does, we should be aware of what our Heavenly Father does so that we can become like Him.

In this lesson you will study...

God Has Character
   The Meaning of God's Character
   The Showing of God's Character
God Is Love
God Is Righteous

This lesson will help you...

- Describe the character of God.
- Appreciate the importance of knowing God's character and how it relates to your life.

GOD HAS CHARACTER

How can you know someone is a person when you meet him? Is it because he looks like a human being? Is it because he talks like a human being? Is it because he walks upright like a human? You *know* someone is a person not just by looks, voice, or movement, but the knowledge and emotions those physical beings express. A person responds and reacts; a person also starts things, because he has ideas and purpose. Yet not all persons seem to be alike. Everyone has his own personality, which is the outward expression of his character.

The Meaning of Character

Objective 1. *Identify the sources from which you can discover God's character.*

God is a person. He does not have a human form, for He is not a man. At the same time, God is not just a power at work in the universe. Certainly it was by His power that the universe was created. But God is more than a power. God has ideas and purposes, intelligence and emotions. He responds and reacts. In all these things, He is far beyond the human beings He created in His image. It seems almost insulting to say that God has a personality, that He is a person. Yet that is the best we can say. And all those qualities which give Him personality are His character. God is wonderful—His character is beyond our understanding. But He has

God is the Pattern For Our Lives

chosen to show His character to us, so that we can be like Him and imitate His ways.

The universe, which God created, shows us something about His unlimited power and intelligence. Paul says:

> Ever since God created the world, his invisible qualities, both his eternal power and his divine nature, have been clearly seen; they are perceived in the things that God has made (Romans 1:20).

But men twisted what they saw to their own desires (Romans 1:21-25). Many religions teach that there is a Creator—God, but they do not have a true understanding of God's character. God Himself has had to make that clear in special ways.

First, God revealed Himself in history to men that He chose. People like Abraham, Moses, Samuel, and Isaiah received special insights into God's nature. The nation of Israel was chosen to demonstrate to men the ways of God. The Old Testament records the knowledge about God that was given to the world in this way. Even though the Old Testament fully describes the character of God, most of mankind remains ignorant of Him.

Also, God revealed His character by sending His Son, Jesus Christ, to live among men.

> In the past, God spoke to our ancestors many times and in many ways through the prophets, but in these last days he has spoken to us through his Son... He reflects the brightness of God's glory and is the exact likeness of God's own being (Hebrews 1:1-3).

For You to Do

1. Which qualities of God's character does creation show you? Circle the letters of the correct answers.
   a God is just a force in nature.
   b God is wise and intelligent.
   c God is cruel.
   d God is all-powerful.

2. Give three sources from which you can discover God's character. The words that you use may not be just like ours, but the ideas should be the same.
   a *God can be known through His creation*
   b *God can be known through the men that He spoke to in the Old Testament*
   c *God can be known through Jesus Christ*

Check your answers with those given at the end of the lesson.

The Showing of God's Character

Objective 2. *Describe how Jesus was able to show you God's character.*

The revelation of God in Jesus, recorded in the New Testament Gospels, in no way contradicts the revelation of God in the Old Testament. Jesus made God's nature, feelings, and actions easier to understand by living them out in the way men could best understand. The Gospel of John calls Jesus "the Word," or revelation, and it says this about Him:

God is the Pattern For Our Lives

> The Word became a human being and, full of grace
> and truth, lived among us. We saw his glory, the
> glory which he received as the Father's only Son
> (John 1:14).

Because Jesus is the Son of God, He was able to tell men about God. Because He shares the nature of God, He was able to show God's character in attitudes and actions.

> No one has ever seen God. The only Son, who is
> the same as God and is at the Father's side, he has
> made him known (John 1:18).

Jesus completed the revelation of God, which even special men were unable to completely understand. He made God's character known to all. What is more, by His death and resurrection, He made available to men the right to become children of God. By the power of His Spirit, God's children are in the process of being changed into the likeness of God. Read what Paul says is happening to you as a believer, as God's child:

> All of us, then, reflect the glory of the Lord with
> uncovered faces; and that same glory, coming from
> the Lord, who is the Spirit, transforms us into his
> likeness in an ever greater degree of glory (2
> Corinthians 3:18).

Glory is the word used in the Bible to describe the wonderful presence of God. Jesus, God's Son, reflected this glory. (See John 1:14.) He shone in this dark world. As you become more and more like God, you too will reflect His glory.

Glory includes all the characteristics of God. The ones which John noticed most in Jesus' glory were *grace* and *truth*. Grace reminds us of the goodness of God, in that He is loving. Truth reminds us of the goodness of God, in that He is the one, true God, holy and righteous. These two parts of God's character affect ethics. God's attitudes and deeds come from His love and from His righteousness.

This illustration shows the characteristics of the glory of God. We can reflect them also in our attitudes and deeds towards others.

For You to Do

3 Memorize this part of 2 Corinthians 3:18: "The Lord, who is the Spirit, transforms us into his likeness in an ever greater degree of glory." Does this not encourage you?

God is the Pattern For Our Lives

4 Pray about how you can cooperate with the Lord as He changes you. You might begin by asking Him to show you, as you study the rest of this lesson, where you are not reflecting His character, His glory.

GOD IS LOVE

Objective 3. *Describe how God's love differs from human love by explaining the meaning of grace and mercy.*

One of the most difficult things for us to understand when we become Christians is how God could have loved us so much that He let His only Son die for us. We are not used to this kind of love. Most of the time the love we see in the world is different. One way to describe the love found in the world is "after me, you come next." This kind of love would say: "If there is enough food for two, I'll share it. If there is only enough for one, I'll eat it." This love takes care of self first, and others second. God's love is so much higher than human love. He is always concerned about what is best for us. He is full of love, even when we don't love Him. He loves the world even when it rejects Him. This kind of love is active. It shows itself in attitude and action, as 1 Corinthians 13:4-7 tells us. In the Bible, God's loving attitude is called *grace* and *mercy*.

Grace is love which shows that it wants the best for another person. Grace does not wait for that person to be good enough to be loved, or to love in return. Grace is an unselfish attitude of pity or compassion. The Lord is "the God of all grace who calls you to share his eternal glory in union with Christ" (1 Peter 5:10).

God's grace is seen because He wants our best when we're sinful. But His love had to become action to rescue us from our sin.

A person shows mercy when he does something for someone who does not deserve it. Do you remember the story of the good Samaritan? It is in Luke 10:30-37. He saw the need of the man who was an enemy. He had pity on him (verse 34) and he helped him, or (to use the King James Version for verse 37) he "had mercy on him."

God has shown grace and mercy to us. He is not like parents who promise, "We'll give you a present, *if* you are good today." God loves without conditions. He wants our best, and provides a way of salvation though we do not deserve it.

For when we were still helpless, Christ died for the wicked at the time that God chose. It is a difficult thing for someone to die for a righteous person. It may even be that someone might dare to die for a good person. But God has shown us how much he loves us—it was while we were still sinners that Christ died for us (Romans 5:6-8).

God's love is neither selfish nor has to be earned. It is free and is so different from human love. God acts differently from men. But God wants to change His children into His likeness. He wants us to reflect His glory and goodness. That means He wants us to love the way He loves, and to show grace and mercy too.

For You to Do

5 Read what Jesus said about loving in Luke 6:27-36. Write the following portions of this passage in your notebook and beside each verse, write one way you can do what the verse says.

Verse 27—Love your enemies, do good to those who hate you.

Verse 36—Be merciful just as your Father is merciful.

GOD IS RIGHTEOUS

Objective 4. *Define "righteous" and tell how God's righteousness is shown in His attitudes and actions.*

At the International Bureau of Weights and Measures in Sèvres, France, there is a bar of special metal. This bar is exactly one meter long. Most countries have a copy of this bar. It is completely *right*. It is the *perfect standard* by which all other lengths are *judged*.

God is like that. By nature He is completely right and good. In every way He is the standard of perfection. All He says or does is true. That is what we mean by saying that God is righteous. He does not change and He does not do any wrong, because those things would be against His nature. God will not be happy with anything less than complete righteousness in those who are to be like Him. Because He is just and true, He has to judge His creation. When God had finished His creative work, the Bible tells us that He was very pleased with it (Genesis 1:31). But you know that men have all sinned; they have failed to stay good and true. Like an imperfect meter ruler, they do not measure up to the standard when they are judged. Paul tells us clearly:

> All have sinned and come short of the glory of God (Romans 3:23, King James Version).

What then could God do? He could not allow men less than true copies of His own righteousness to be near Him, could He?

Imagine you wanted to build a table. Four friends offered to bring wood for the legs. You gave them each the right measurement. When they arrived, you used your ruler and saw that each leg was short. One was

God is the Pattern For Our Lives

short by 10 centimeters, one by 5, one by 3, and one by 2. Which can you use just as it is? None, if you want a table of the right height which will not fall over!

God measures, or judges, the shortcomings of men. Not just because men do bad things, but because they do not show love and mercy as He does.

There is a story of a very good judge who demanded truth and justice, not clever use of laws. One day his son was brought before him for a crime that he had committed. The son admitted that he was indeed guilty. With tears of love the judge sentenced him to prison—for justice demands punishment. Then the judge rose, took off his robes, and stepped down to where his son stood. He spoke to the guards and said, "I will serve the prison sentence for my son."

As God's child, you are not condemned with the world. Jesus has taken your place and met God's justice. Now God's justice has set you free. For this reason you should be true and righteous also—with the power of the Holy Spirit.

When we understand that God's love and righteousness are both a part of His nature, then we can begin to see how these attitudes affect what He does for us. We can also begin to see how God expects us to think, to feel, to act, so we can become more like Him.

> The Lord has told us what is good. What he requires of us is this: to do what is just, to show constant love, and to live in humble fellowship with our God (Micah 6:8).

For You to Do

6 Write Micah 6:8 in your notebook and memorize it.

7 Read Ephesians 5:8-10 in your Bible. Then list in your notebook things which you have learned God expects you to do now that you are His child.

8 When we say God is righteous we mean
  a) He can be measured.
  b) He does not do wrong.
  c) He is too good to listen to us.

(b is circled)

9 How can God's righteousness affect your attitudes and actions?

He can help you not do wrong, have a better attitude, show constant love, and have humble fellowship with Him.

Check Your Answers

5 Your answer.

1 **b** God is wise and intelligent.
  d God is all-powerful.

6 Your answer.

2 **a** God can be known through His creation.
  b God can be known through the men to whom He spoke as recorded in the Old Testament.
  c God can be known through Jesus Christ.

7 Your answer.

3 Your answer.

8 b) He does not do wrong.

4 Your answer.

9 He can help you not do wrong, have a better attitude, show constant love, and have humble fellowship with Him.

Lesson 3: What God Wants You to Be and Do

Have you learned to ride a bicycle? If so, you know that as a learner you had to remember to do many things at the same time. You had to push the pedals and guide the handlebars, while keeping your balance and obeying the rules of the road. These are things that the expert rider does without thinking, but you couldn't do them.

How then did you learn to ride? Most likely you had an expert rider helping you. Probably he explained to you what you had to do and how to obey the rules of the road. Perhaps he got on the bicycle and showed you what to do. When you had to try for yourself did you fall down? Because he understood, the expert probably then helped you by holding on to the bicycle until you developed a sense of balance like his.

Learning to live as God wants is like this. God desires that we all become like Him, and you know that He is good, loving, and righteous. But we can't just start living that way on our own when we become Christians. This lesson shows how God, the expert, can take you, tell you, show you, and help you become more and more like Him.

In this lesson you will study...

A Conscience to Help You
The Bible to Guide You
A Savior to Show You
The Holy Spirit to Lead You

This lesson will help you...

- Identify the ways God uses to show you how to live.
- Make better use of the helps God has given you for living a more responsible life.
- Name four ways you can be sure of making the right choices in life.

A CONSCIENCE TO HELP YOU

Objective 1. *Define conscience and describe its part in helping you become a better Christian.*

All men have a conscience. It is an inner awareness about what is good and right. Even before you became a Christian, your conscience gave you some guidance about what was right and wrong. You had a feeling inside and you knew that you should or should not do a certain act. If you took notice of your conscience, you avoided many sinful deeds and perhaps did many right deeds. The apostle Paul explains this when he talks of the Gentiles, who did not know God's laws, doing good because of those inner feelings. He says:

> Their conduct shows that what the Law commands is written in their hearts. Their consciences also show that this is true, since their thoughts sometimes accuse them and sometimes defend them (Romans 2:15).

Conscience is good. It is a gift of God to help us. We might say that it is a spiritual sense of balance. But like our natural sense of balance, which helps us walk or ride a bicycle, our conscience is limited and imperfect. The best acrobat or rider sometimes falls because his sense of balance fails. Just so, the best of men fall into sin because their conscience is not sufficient to hold them. Some men make their conscience useless by time after time refusing to listen to it. They are like men who ignore a good road and make their own crooked paths; in the end, the road is covered with weeds and they cannot use it when they want to. The Bible talks of people "whose consciences are dead, as if burnt with a hot iron" (1 Timothy 4:2).

Christians are not like that. When they are born again, their misused conscience is made new again. The writer to the Hebrews encourages us, by showing that Christ's death makes our conscience right.

> His blood will purify our consciences from useless rituals, so that we may serve the living God (Hebrews 9:14).

Because Christ purifies our heart and forgives us, our conscience does not make us feel guilty about past sins any more.

Instead, our conscience becomes a tool of the Holy Spirit to assure us that we are acting rightly. The writer to the Hebrews asks for prayer, saying:

> Keep on praying for us. We are sure we have a clear conscience, because we want to do the right thing at all times (Hebrews 13:18).

Your conscience will help you to do good deeds, by warning you when you are thinking of doing bad and giving you peace when you want to do good. A quiet conscience is a clear conscience (1 Peter 3:16). Paul's advice to Timothy is a great encouragement and a strong warning:

> Keep your faith and a clear conscience. Some men have not listened to their conscience and have made a ruin of their faith (1 Timothy 1:19).

For You to Do

1 Circle the letter for the TRUE statements about conscience.
  a Only non-Christians have consciences.
  b Christ renews the Christian's conscience.
  c A renewed conscience is a tool of the Holy Spirit.
  d Conscience can never be wrong.
  e A Christian should keep a clear conscience.

2 Write the following verse in your notebook, memorize it, and use it as a guide. When you must make a decision to do something or not do it, ask yourself which action allows you to have a clear conscience.

I do my best always to have a clear conscience before God and man (Acts 24:16).

Check your answers with those given at the end of the lesson.

THE BIBLE TO GUIDE YOU

Objective 2. *Describe how the Bible is your guide in living a Christian life.*

In the last lesson you learned about the Bible as part of the way God revealed Himself. You remember that the Old Testament records God's dealings with individual men and with the nation of Israel. God chose to show His character and His way in that manner. The

New Testament contains an account of the way God revealed Himself most fully—in Jesus Christ. The Gospels tell the story of Jesus and give His teaching. Acts continues the story; the Epistles explain the teaching; Revelation speaks of the victorious end of the story.

When the Bible has so many important things to tell us, it is easy to see why we need the whole Scripture. Yet many people, even Christians, do not understand why God has made His Word available to us today. The Bible itself gives the best answer:

> All Scripture is inspired by God and is useful for teaching the truth, rebuking error, correcting faults, and giving instruction for right living (2 Timothy 3:16).

The Scriptures are given by God and they are therefore useful to us. Their use is to teach us the truth, the right things about the true God and our new life in Christ. That way, we will not be ignorant and make mistakes—we can ask for God's help to put wrong things right in our lives. The clear teaching of the Bible will guide us in the right ways of living.

All the knowledge of the Bible is of little use if we do not let it change our attitudes and actions to be like God's. On the other hand, desiring to help God change our lives is of little use either, unless we listen to and understand the Word of God.

The Psalmist had a great respect for the Word of God. He said:

> Your word is a lamp to guide me and a light for my path. I will keep my solemn promise to obey your just instructions (Psalm 119:105-106).

The Bible is the all-sufficient guide for our Christian path in life. That is why we must continually see what the Scriptures say when we have questions about our way of being, feeling, and doing.

The Bible contains instructions. These are very definite rules to be obeyed. The Bible also gives patterns of behavior. These help us decide how to act, without telling us exactly what to do.

Finally, the Bible gives us examples: real people obeying or rebelling against God's rules and fellowship and accepting or rejecting God's patterns. There is never any doubt which God wants us to copy. The good inspire us to deeds which please God; the bad warn us against feelings and actions which would displease God.

The Word of God is very practical—it deals with reality. If we are to live our life God's way, we have to be practical and know God's Word. Knowing God's

What God Wants You to Be and Do 49

Word requires a desire to obey and discipline to study, but it is the way to true happiness in life.

> I delight in following your commands more than in having great wealth. I study your instructions; I examine your teachings. I take pleasure in your laws; your commands I will not forget (Psalms 119:14-16).

For You to Do

3 Circle the letter in front of each TRUE statement.
  a) The Bible is inspired by God for your good.
  b) The Bible is useful for teaching the truth.
  c) The Bible is given to equip the Christian to deal with life.
  d The Bible is only a list of things you must not do.
  e) The Bible is full of good instructions and patterns for living.

4 Take one of the three Scripture passages given in this section and write it in your notebook. Memorize it and study it so that you can explain to anyone who asks you why the Bible is such an important guide for your Christian living.

A SAVIOR TO SHOW YOU

Objective 3. *Explain how Jesus is your example as well as your Lord and Savior.*

The most valuable example that the Bible offers us is our Lord Jesus Christ. Probably you tell others that Jesus is your Savior. Perhaps you think of Him constantly as your Lord. These are right and good. How could you have experienced new life without salvation? How could you go on living without the Lord in control? *Only Jesus* is able to save and keep, when we ask Him into ours hearts. Jesus is *Christ*, and you are a *Christian*. That word means that you are a follower of Christ, one of His disciples. A disciple is one who learns to think and act like his master.

Did you ever play a game called "Follow the Leader"? One person does a series of actions—jumping, bending, walking—and the others have to do their best to copy his movements. If you can not copy him, or are the slowest to do so, then you lose. That game is built on imitation. The Bible teaches us to imitate our Lord:

> Imitate me, then, just as I imitate Christ (1 Corinthians 11:1).

The attitude you should have is the one that Christ Jesus had: He was humble and walked the path of obedience (Philippians 2:5, 8).

Jesus showed His character by His actions while He walked the path of obedience. Peter summed this up when he preached that Jesus "went everywhere, doing good and healing ... for God was with Him" (Acts 10:38). Peter knew Jesus' character because he had been with Him.

> The members of the Council were amazed to see how bold Peter and John were and to learn that

What God Wants You to Be and Do

they were ordinary men of no education. They realized then that they had been companions of Jesus (Acts 4:13).

You see what is meant about reading your Bible? It is not just to know the stories of Jesus that you read the Gospels. You need to read the Bible to be able to know the ways of Jesus and to copy them, by the power of God's Spirit within you. It won't be easy. Jesus did not live an easy life either. In fact, He suffered many things for our sake. Peter knew that when he said:

> It was to this that God called you, for Christ himself suffered for you and left you an example, so that you would follow in his steps (1 Peter 2:21).

Now you know that you should imitate Jesus. He is so wonderful. Can you ever hope to be like Him? God certainly wants us to become more like Him every day, but like Paul we know we are not up to His standard yet (Philippians 3:12). But we will be! Here is a marvelous promise to God's children and to you:

> My dear friends, we are now God's children, but it is not yet clear what we shall become. But we know that when Christ appears, we shall be like him,

because we shall see him as he really is. Everyone who has this hope in Christ keeps himself pure, just as Christ is pure (1 John 3:2-3).

For You to Do

5 Circle the letters of the statements below which describe things we should do to imitate Jesus.
a) We must love God with all our heart.
b) We must tell the good news to the poor.
c) We must help those who are in trouble.
d) We must let the Spirit of God work in us.
e We must all become carpenters.

6 Read 1 Corinthians 11:1 again. Pray asking the Holy Spirit to show you ways in which others can imitate you, because you are imitating Christ. Then ask the Holy Spirit to show you ways in which you are not yet imitating Christ. Ask God to forgive you and help you change. List these in your notebook and pray each day that you may become more and more like Jesus. When the Holy Spirit has helped you change where you were not imitating Christ, draw a line through it and write what He has helped you learn.

THE HOLY SPIRIT TO LEAD YOU

Objective 4. *Describe the work of the Holy Spirit in leading you into a more Christlike life.*

There are many people in the world who know many facts about Jesus. They have memorized them from the Bible. But they are unable to copy Jesus in their lives. Somehow, they have not seen the need to become Christians by asking Jesus to be their Savior. That is like trying to ride the bicycle without ever getting on it. There is no way that you can do it without trying. To become like Jesus, you have to first become a child of God.

Many of God's children have never made any progress in becoming Christlike. They do not seem to be able to keep away from the same old sins and the same bad habits. They repent sincerely, but they continue to fall. They are like the new rider who cannot stop falling off his bicycle. Why? Because he is unable to keep his balance without help, the help of his expert teacher.

Thank God that there is an expert teacher available to help us. If we are God's child, our teacher is within us. He is the Holy Spirit of God. God's Spirit is our faithful friend and helper. How can we fail then? By refusing to let the Spirit help us. We need to ask Him each day to hold us just like the teacher holds the learner's bike. Then we will go forward with confidence becoming more and more like Jesus each day.

The disciples of Jesus were His followers for three years. Jesus taught them many things and showed them His example. But He knew that when He went away, they would need help. So He made a promise:

> The Helper will come—the Spirit, who reveals the truth about God and who comes from the Father. I will send him to you from the Father, and he will speak about me (John 15:26).

Our Helper is inside us to reveal more about God the Father and God the Son. He helps us by instructing us. He takes the words of the Bible and makes them more real to us. As Jesus said a little earlier:

> The Helper, the Holy Spirit, whom the Father will send in my name, will teach you everything and make you remember all that I have told you (John 14:26).

The Holy Spirit teaches, but He also reminds us of what we have learned. He brings the Scriptures to our mind when we need them. When we are in difficult circumstances, He tells us what to say (Mark 13:11). His job is to lead us into all the truth (John 16:13), and that includes the way we are to live. As we let the Spirit help us, we can overcome the desires of our human nature. We can let God's nature show itself in us, but only as we follow the Holy Spirit's leading and helping hand on us. Read carefully what the apostle Paul wrote about this:

> But the Spirit produces love, joy, peace, patience, kindness, goodness, faithfulness, humility, and self-control. There is no law against such things as these.

> The Spirit has given us life; he must also control our lives (Galatians 5:22-23, 25).

The Holy Spirit must *control* our lives. Does that mean we don't have to make any effort? Of course not! It means that we must not keep trying to avoid God's way. We must think about our attitudes and actions, and ask the Spirit to change them to be like Christ's. That is His *leading* into all truth.

Does this seem hard to you? Consider for a moment what God has already done in you. It was the Holy Spirit who helped you become a Christian. The Spirit gave you *life*. By His power you became a child of God. You experienced that God was real and He forgave your sins. Your conscience was renewed. You were given a purpose for living. Every day God your Father is answering your prayers. Because of all this you are learning more and more what God is like. All this because the Holy Spirit is working in you! And not only in you, but in all your Christian brothers and sisters.

We have no cause to fear that we will fail. What the Bible tells us, we can also know by personal experience:

> Those who are led by God's Spirit are God's sons. For the Spirit that God has given you does not make you slaves and cause you to be afraid; instead, the Spirit makes you God's children, and by the spirit's power we cry out to God, "Father! my Father!" God's Spirit joins himself to our spirits to declare that we are God's children (Romans 8:14-16).

For You to Do

7 Look at the Scriptures used in this section. Then after each statement below, write the scripture reference that tells us this truth.

  a The Spirit leads us.
  8:14

  b The Spirit has given us life.
  5:25

  c The Spirit reveals the truth about God.
  15:26

  d The Spirit helps us remember Christ's words.
  14:26

  e The Spirit produces a Christlike character in us.
  5:22-23

8 Paul prayed this prayer and we pray it for you also. Write your name on the blank spaces, and pray it yourself.

I .. John Brunzell... ask the God of our Lord Jesus Christ, the glorious Father, to give John Brunzell. the Spirit, who will make John Brunzell. wise and reveal God to John Brunzell. so that John Brunzell....'s mind may be opened to see the light ... and how very great is His power at work in us who believe (Ephesians 1:17-19).

Check Your Answers

5 a We must love God with all our heart.
  b We must tell the good news to the poor.
  c We must help those who are in trouble.
  d We must let the Spirit of God work in us.

1 b Christ renews the Christian's conscience.
  c A renewed conscience is a tool of the Holy Spirit.
  e A Christian should keep a clear conscience.

6 Your answer.

2 Your answer.

7 a Romans 8:14.
  b Galatians 5:25.
  c John 15:26.
  d John 14:26.
  e Galatians 5:22-23.

3 a True.
  b True.
  c True.
  d False.
  e True.

8 Your name goes on the blanks.

4 Your answer.

Lesson 4

God Gives You Rules for Living

This month we have to get new driving licenses. To do that we must first pass a test on the signs and rules which car drivers need to know. Right before us on our desk is a booklet called "Rules of the Road." These rules are good. If we follow them, we will not have as many accidents. We will also not have problems with the policemen who make sure that the laws of the country are obeyed. Sometimes we might wish to drive faster than the speed limit. But, the rules on speeding are made to discourage us from doing what could be dangerous. These rules were made to help keep us out of trouble and to prevent us from harming others.

We have rules in our family too. For instance, our children may not play with a ball in the house. Children need rules. A child will feel more secure if he knows what he should and should not do. If he disobeys a rule; he must be punished. Discipline is good if it is done in love. It teaches a child that everyone will always be happier if rules are followed.

God, the Creator of all men, has rules too. He desires that His children know and follow all of His rules. That is why He revealed His rules through Moses and through His Son Jesus Christ.

In this lesson you will study..

Rules of Men
Commandments of God by Moses
Teachings of Jesus
Apostles' Directions

This lesson will help you...

- Identify the important rules God has given in the Bible.
- Appreciate that the rules that Jesus gave show what we are to be like rather than what we are not supposed to do.

RULES OF MEN

Objective 1. *Explain how God wants you to feel about the leaders and the rules of your country.*

God's rules have to do with order in society. God desires that people and familes should live together in peace and harmony. He has allowed men to develop their political systems. We may live in a tribe with a chief, a monarchy with a king, or a republic with a president. There are leaders who make the rules, or laws, which govern our society. Not all leaders or laws are good in God's sight, but He wants us to respect them.

The apostle Paul tells us this in Romans 13:1-3:

> Everyone must obey state authorities, because no authority exists without God's permission, and the existing authorities have been put there by God. Whoever opposes the existing authority opposes what God has ordered; and anyone who does so will bring judgment on himself. For rulers are not to be feared by those who do good, but by those who do evil (Romans 13:1-3).

Authorities exist to control evil and to punish those who break the laws. Paul says that because laws punish evil, they act as God's servants. We must obey them not only out of fear but "as a matter of conscience" (Romans 13:5).

Paul then goes on to talk about paying taxes as a matter of conscience:

That is also why you pay taxes, because the authorities are working for God when they fulfill their duties. Pay, then, what you owe them; pay them your personal and property taxes, and show respect and honor for them all (Romans 13:6-7).

Christians owe first duty to the Kingdom of God. As free citizens of the heavenly kingdom, we must be good examples to unbelievers by our obedience to the authorities by paying our taxes. Peter encourages us: "For the sake of the Lord submit yourselves to every human authority" (1 Peter 2:13).

Jesus is a wonderful example of obeying authority. Though He was King of Kings, He paid taxes so as not to offend people (see Matthew 17:24-27). When enemies tried to trap Him with a question about taxes, Jesus gave this good advice:

Pay to the Emperor what belongs to the Emperor, and pay to God what belongs to God (Matthew 22:21).

For You to Do

1 Circle the letters before all the TRUE statements about the Christian's attitude toward his government.

~~F~~ **a** He resents paying taxes because he is God's child.
T **b** He desires to obey the laws of his country.
T **c** He pays taxes out of conscience.
T **d** He respects human authorities.
T **e** He puts the law of God above human laws.

2 Write Matthew 22:21 in your notebook. Can you think of some examples of what you have that belongs to your government and what belongs to God? Some of your examples may belong to both. Make a list of the things you have thought of.

Check your answers with those at the end of this lesson.

COMMANDMENTS OF GOD BY MOSES

Objective 2. *Show that you know what God's laws are, and why it is important to have the help of the Holy Spirit in order to obey them.*

Human laws may be good or bad. They serve the society for which they were made. God's law is perfectly good and suited for all men everywhere. The Psalmist exclaimed:

> You are righteous, Lord, and your laws are just. The rules that you have given are completely fair and right (Psalm 119:137-138).

God gave laws to His people through His servant Moses. Many men believed in God and understood something of His ways. But most people did not know God's rules. God then revealed His perfect law to the Hebrew nation whom He had chosen when He gave His commandments to Moses on the mountain called Sinai. You can read the story and all God said to Moses in Exodus 19—31. The first and most important rules are called the Ten Commandments.

In Deuteronomy 5, Moses told these rules to the people so that they would learn and obey them (verse 1). He wanted them to know that they were the basis of God's covenant with them. God would continue to bless them if they did not disobey the laws (verses 32-33).

Even though we are God's people of the new covenant through Jesus' death, we should still know and keep the Ten Commandments. They are for all men. Without them we cannot have a healthy, prosperous, or good society. Let's look at them briefly:

1. Worship no god but the Lord.
2. Make no images to worship.
3. Do not use God's name for evil purposes.

4. Observe God's day of rest.
5. Respect your father and mother.
6. Do not commit murder.
7. Do not commit adultery.
8. Do not steal.
9. Do not accuse anyone falsely.
10. Do not desire another man's wife or what he owns.

God gave these rules to help us live in peace and prosperity. He gave them because He is a kind and loving Father.

> Remember that the Lord your God corrects and punishes you just as a father disciplines his children. So then, do as the Lord has commanded you: live according to his laws and have reverence for him (Deuteronomy 8:5-6).

The nation of Israel did not always follow these laws, and they were punished. But they were no worse than other people. Every man and woman has sinned against God by breaking one or more of the Ten Commandments. Even the most religious men have failed at some point.

A fine religious young man came to Jesus one day (Mark 10:17-22). He wanted to know what he must do to receive eternal life. Jesus questioned him about the last five commandments and this man proudly said he had kept them all. Then Jesus lovingly challenged him to give away all his wealth and to follow Him. The Bible says that the young man went away sad because he was very rich. We imagine that he loved riches more than

obedience to God's Son. Wealth was his god, not the Lord. Without realizing it, he was breaking the first commandment.

Indeed God has high standards of conduct for His people. None of us can fulfill all the laws of God by ourselves. The apostle Paul expresses our problem in Romans 7:21-25: though we know God's laws to be right and desire to do good, we cannot overcome our human nature. Happily God has the answer to our problem!

> What the Law could not do, because human nature was weak, God did. He condemned sin in human nature by sending his own Son, who came with a nature like man's sinful nature, to do away with sin. God did this so that the righteous demands of the Law might be fully satisfied in us who live according to the Spirit, and not according to human nature (Romans 8:3-4).

Jesus, Son of Man and Son of God, fulfilled all God's commandments (Matthew 5:17). Through His death we are forgiven for our failures, and through His Spirit we learn to obey God's laws.

For You to Do

3 Write out Psalm 119:33-35 in your notebook. Learn it and make it your personal prayer.

Keep me obedient to your commandments, because in them I find happiness. Give me the desire to obey your laws rather than to get rich. Keep me from paying attention to what is worthless; be good to me, as you have promised (Psalm 119:35-37).

4 Circle all of the letters before the statements which describe the laws of God.
   ⓐ God's rules are perfect.
   b All the laws given to Moses were only for the Hebrews.
   c Men can easily obey all the Ten Commandments.
   ⓓ God gave His rules to help men live right.
   e The Ten Commandments are out-of-date.
   ⓕ Jesus obeyed all God's laws.
   ⓖ We need the Holy Spirit to help us obey these rules.

God Gives You Rules for Living 67

5 If you have not already learned the Ten Commandments, write them in your notebook and memorize them. As you are learning them, ask the Holy Spirit to help you obey them.

TEACHINGS OF JESUS

Objective 3. *Tell why the law of Christ is called the law of love.*

A teacher once came to Jesus and asked Him a difficult question about God's laws: "Which is the greatest commandment in the Law?" (Matthew 22:36). Jesus did not choose one of the Ten Commandments. Instead he chose from the Old Testament a command of God which includes the first four commandments:

> Love the Lord your God with all your heart, with all your soul, and with all your strength (Deuteronomy 6:5).

You see, if you love God you will worship Him only, you will not misuse His name, you will do everything to please Him. Love will be the motive behind your obedience to all the laws. That is why Jesus, in His answer to the teacher, added a second great command found in the Old Testament. This command includes the last five commandments:

> Love your neighbor as you love yourself (Leviticus 19:18).

If you love your neighbor you won't kill him, take his wife or his property. You will want the very best in life for him. That's what love is like, and this love is the fruit of the Spirit. Love is shown by the actions of the Spirit-filled Christian.

When Jesus was ready to leave His disciples, He was careful to give them instructions. Jesus loved His disciples and they loved Him. He told them: "If you love me, you will obey my commandments" (John 14:15). He promised to send a "Helper," the Holy Spirit, to teach them how to obey (John 14:16-17, 26). Then He told them:

> My commandment is this: love one another, just as I love you. The greatest love a person can have for his friends is to give his life for them (John 15:12-13).

The love of Jesus is practical. He did something for us: He gave His life to save us. Now His rule for all His disciples is that they should **do** something too. The apostle Paul understood that when he wrote:

> Help carry one another's burdens, and in this way you will obey the law of Christ (Galatians 6:2).

God Gives You Rules for Living

We are to show our love for our Lord by doing good deeds for others. You remember in Lesson 1 that the intention of God for His children was to do good deeds? Now we see that it is the commandment of Jesus.

Love that works is a central rule of the Kingdom of God. But we saw that the character of God is more than love. He is also righteous. Love that works must be directed in the right way. Jesus gave much teaching on love and on righteousness. The Sermon on the Mount, found in Matthew 5-7, tells us about some of this teaching.

In this sermon, Jesus told His disciples about the high standards of righteousness they were to aim at. They were not just to refrain from evil actions. They were not even to have evil thoughts! For example, Jesus says that obeying the commandment about not committing adultery is not enough. His disciples must not even have the wrong thoughts (Matthew 5:27-28). Jesus is not satisfied if we do good things just for our friends. No, He tells us to also love our enemies and pray for them "so that you may become the sons of your Father in heaven" (Matthew 5:43-45).

The commandments of Jesus mean a new way of life. Our giving, and praying must be done privately, not to "show off." We are to do everything for God's sake, not for the praise of men. We are to do things which are not hypocritical, that is, good only in appearance. Jesus tells His disciples over and over that God is interested in motives and attitudes, as well as deeds.

The teachings of Jesus are *positive*. He does not list things we must *not* do. He tells us how to go beyond laws which say "Do not." He tells us to love God, to love and to do good to our neighbor because we love Him. He commands us:

> Be concerned above everything else with the Kingdom of God and with what he requires of you (Matthew 6:33).

For You To Do

6 What Jesus tells us to do is sometimes different from what our human nature would want. Circle the letter before each commandment given in the Sermon on the Mount for which you need the help of the Holy Spirit.
a) Be glad when you are persecuted.
b) Avoid taking revenge when someone wrongs you.
c) Love your enemies.
d) Make your gifts of charity a private matter.
e) Forgive others when they wrong you.
f) Refrain from judging other people.

7 Which of these commands do you have the most problem with? Write it in your notebook and pray for God's help to obey Jesus' command. Leave a space to write down how the Holy Spirit helps you to obey the command this week.

APOSTLES' DIRECTIONS

Objective 4. *List ways in which Christ's law of love can be applied in practical, daily living, as presented in the apostles' teaching.*

After Jesus went to be with the Father, His apostles went out to preach the good news of salvation to all people everywhere. Some were Jews; they understood that God was holy and had given the laws to help them avoid sins. They learned easily the law of love which Jesus gave. But other people were from countries which did not understand the character of God. The apostles had to teach them more basic teaching. These people had their own religions and had to learn a new way of life. Their old way was evil and the apostles had to teach them the commands of Jesus.

We find the teaching of the apostles in the Bible. They taught as Jesus taught. They told the people how the commands of the Lord could help them with their problems. For example, John the apostle taught the command to believe in Jesus and love one another. He told Christian believers:

> My children, our love should not be just words and talk; it must be true love, which shows itself in action (1 John 3:18).

James, writing to "all God's people scattered over the whole world" (James 1:1), had the same concern. He encouraged everyone to do the right thing, by obeying "the law of the Kingdom" (James 2:8), which is the command to love your neighbor. Then he applied it to their lives: "But if you treat people according to their outward appearance, you are guilty of sin" (James 2:9). Discrimination—liking or hating a person because of his race, sex, or social status—is against the law of love. Christianity changes our attitudes toward people, and what we do to help them. The book of James says:

> What God the Father considers to be pure and genuine religion is this: to take care of orphans and widows in their suffering and to keep oneself from being corrupted by the world (James 1:27).

The apostle Paul had been a slave to the rules of man before he became a Christian. He realized that they could not save him; salvation is not the result of our own efforts (read Ephesians 2:8-9). Yet when we have accepted the gift of salvation through Jesus Christ, we are responsible for living a new kind of life. Paul warns us:

> Do not continue to live like the heathen, whose thoughts are worthless and whose minds are in the dark. They have no part in the life that God gives, for they are completely ignorant and stubborn.
>
> Your hearts and minds must be made completely new, and you must put on the new self, which is created in God's likeness and reveals itself in the true life that is upright and holy (Ephesians 4:17-18, 23-24).

Paul gives many words of advice in Ephesians. Here are a few of his helpful directions for living the Christian life by the power of the Spirit. You can find them in Ephesians 4, 5, and 6.

God Gives You Rules for Living

1. Be always humble, gentle, and patient.
2. Show your love by being tolerant with each other.
3. No more lying! Tell the truth.
4. Stop robbing and start working.
5. Help the poor.
6. Do not use harmful words but only helpful words.
7. No bitterness or anger; be kind and tender-hearted.
8. Forgive one another.
9. No sexual immorality or indencency or greed.
10. Try to learn what pleases the Lord.
11. Do not get drunk with wine but be filled with the Spirit.
12. Always give thanks for everything to God.
13. Submit yourselves to one another.
14 Wives, submit to your husbands as to the Lord.
15. Husbands, love your wives just as Christ loved the Church.
16. Children, obey your parents.
17. Parents, do not treat your children in such a way as to make them angry; raise them with Christian discipline and instruction.
18. Put on all the armor of God.
19. Pray on every occasion, as the Spirit leads.

What wonderful directions! This is not a list of what not to do. It is a positive and active list of good deeds we can do. We must stop doing bad things to be able to do the good things! Doing better things will not only make us happier, it will make us more like our Heavenly Father. That, as Paul reminds us, is the purpose of living our lives by the law of love:

> Since you are God's dear children, you must try to be like him. Your life must be controlled by love, just as Christ loved us and gave his life for us as a sweet-smelling offering and sacrifice that pleases God (Ephesians 5:1-2).

For You To Do

8 Circle the letter before each of these actions which obey the law of love.
   a Beating your child because he walks slowly
   b Giving food to a family where there is sickness
   c Helping a man find a job
   d Cursing a driver whose car almost struck you
   e Praying for your pastors
   f Respecting the elders of your community

9 All of us have areas in our lives where we do not obey the law of love. Pray and ask the Holy Spirit to show you the ways in which you have not obeyed the law of love, and ask God to help you to change.

10 Draw the chart shown in your notebook. At the top of each column write the titles: "Living with Myself," "Living with My Family," "Living in My Community," "Living in My Church." For two weeks write the ways in which you obey the law of love. You will see that the second week is easier than the first.

God Gives You Rules for Living

Living with Myself	Living with My Family	Living in My Community	Living in My Church

Now that you have completed the first four lessons, you are ready to answer the first section of your student report. Review Lessons 1-4, then follow the instructions in your student report. When you send your answer sheets to your instructor, ask him about another course of study.

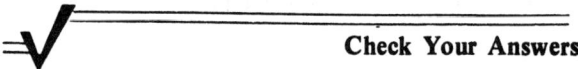
Check Your Answers

6 All are beyond our natural ability, and so all require the help of the Holy Spirit.

1 a False.
  b True.
  c True.
  d True.
  e True.

7 Your answer.

2 Your list may be different from ours, but here are some examples:

Government—taxes, serving in the army
God—tithes, serving God in church work

8 b Giving food to a family where there is sickness
c Helping a man find a job
e Praying for your pastors
f Respecting the elders of your community

3 Your answer.

9 Your answer.

4 a God's rules are perfect.
d God gave His rules to help men live right.
f Jesus obeyed all God's laws.
g We need the Holy Spirit to help us obey these rules.

10 Your answer. As you continue to obey the law of love God will make you happier.

5 Your answer.

Lesson 5: God Gives You Standards for Living

Let us imagine that you are considering buying a bicycle. In the shop you see a beautiful shining bicycle. You have always wanted a bicycle just like it. Of course you want it. Because you are a child of God though, you do not act without thinking first. You do not immediately take all your family's money, or borrow from your friends and buy it. As a child of God, you know you should make a wise decision. So what do you do?

The Bible does not have any verse telling you "You *must* buy this bicycle" or "You *must not* buy this bicycle. There were no bicycles in Bible days. Besides, buying a bicycle is neither a good or a bad action. So God does not have a rule about buying bicycles.

Is the Bible of no help then in making these decisions? Of course it helps—the Bible helps us "to do every kind of good deed" (2 Timothy 3:17) and that includes making decisions. The Bible is not a magical object which tells us yes or no for every decision. It is a guide to use, for God has given us the right to make decisions. He treats us as His children, not as His slaves just to be ordered about!

The Bible does instruct us on making decisions though. In this lesson we will learn about the principles or standards which are found in Scripture. These principles can help us as we face difficult decisions in our daily lives.

In this lesson you will study...

Principles are Standards to Live By
Finding Biblical Principles
   The Principle of Stewardship
   The Principle of Service
Applying Biblical Principles

This lesson will help you....

- Identify guidelines by which you may make good decisions in your Christian life.

- Determine the importance of using proper values in daily living by studying your Bible

PRINCIPLES ARE STANDARDS TO LIVE BY

Objective 1. *Explain the difference between Biblical principles and principles of the world.*

Rules tell you what you may or may not do. They can show you what actions are wrong. Principles are more like measuring sticks. They help you to know whether one possible action is better, as good, or worse than another. For example, the principles you use can help you decide whether to buy the new bicycle, a used bicycle, or no bicycle at all.

We all act by principles, although most people do not realize it. The most common principle is that of selfish pleasure which means, "If something pleases me, makes me feel good, then I will do it." If you follow this principle, you would buy the new bicycle without considering what would happen. Perhaps your family would starve because you used the money intended for food. Perhaps you would be in great debt.

By doing this, you would have satisfied your own selfishness. Maybe nothing bad would happen as a result of your selfish action. Perhaps buying the bicycle would help you in your job or ministry. But in making your decision you did not consider how it would help. Your standard for living was to please yourself. It is not the standard that Jesus lived and died by. If you have a Bible, turn to Philippians 2 and read what Paul has to say about Christ's humility and greatness.

God Gives You Standards for Living

Another standard by which people decide what to do is the principle of popularity. *Popularity* means "liked by most people" and always includes wanting the praise of men. People like you for having the things or position they admire. Let's go back to our buying the new bicycle. Perhaps all the men you work with have new bicycles, and you hate to be different. Perhaps your neighbors have old bicycles or no bicycles at all, and you want to be better than they are. Perhaps owning a bicycle like that would give you good influence in your neighborhood, and that is what you want. The Bible tells us to desire the praise of God rather than man (Romans 2:29). Wanting only to be popular with men is not a Christian principle.

Of course we could go on and on. Men have many reasons for their actions: laziness, pride, and desire for power. What we must do now is discover in the Bible the principles by which Christians must live.

For You To Do

1 When making a decision about buying something special, think first about what
a) would make you popular with the people you know.
b) reason you have for needing it and then pray before making your decision.
c) you want to have and buy it right away.

2 Think about a recent decision you made. Can you tell what principle or principles you were using? Would your decision have been different if you had used another princple?

Check your answers with those given at the end of the lesson.

FINDING BIBLICAL PRINCIPLES

Objective 2. *Give an example of a simple method that can be followed for finding biblical principles.*

Biblical principles all come from the great law of love. This law of love means Christians are to live in such a way that they show love: to God the Father, to other men and women, and to themselves because God loves them. The biblical principle of love includes many other principles. It will be helpful for you to find the biblical principles which can help you make your decisions. Then, when you have questions about how you should act in each situation you will have the biblical principle you need.

God Gives You Standards for Living

How do you find which biblical principles apply? Here are three ways of finding them in the Bible:

1. Look at the biblical examples of behavior that God wants us to have or not to have. For example, the story of the Good Samaritan who showed kindness to his neighbor and Jesus said, "You go, then, and do the same" (Luke 10:37). Showing kindness is a good standard to live by.

2. Study the explanations and suggestions given in the Bible about Christian living. The Bible gives us many stories and commands which help us live good Christian lives. For example, the Scripture says, "He gives generously to the needy" (2 Corinthians 9:9). This principle and others like it explain what we are to *do* to live right.

3. Above all, look carefully at the way Jesus our Lord acted. If we are to become more like Him we must know what He lived like, "The attitude you should have is the one that Christ Jesus had" (Philippians 2:5).

Using the methods listed, you should be able to find the principles which can help you with all of life's problems. Remember, however, that these biblical principles are God's. They develop wisdom which God gives to His children through His Word. We can only find His wisdom through Bible study and by prayer. Finding His wisdom is a biblical principle in itself: to be wise you must be humble, obedient, and patient. The Epistle of James says:

> If any of you lacks wisdom, he should pray to God, who will give it to him (James 1:5).

This verse teaches first that we must be *humble*. To be *humble* we need to admit to God that we do not know all the answers. At the same time, we must believe that God does have the answer. Second, when we pray we are *obedient*. We come to our Father like Jesus said to do:

> Let us be brave, then, and approach God's throne, where there is grace. There we will receive mercy and find grace to keep us just when we need it (Hebrews 4:16).

Finally, you should expect to receive the answer. Wait until you are sure that God has given you His will. Search the Scriptures and let the Holy Spirit give you direction for making your decision.

God Gives You Standards for Living

For You To Do

3 One way of finding the biblical principle that will help you make a decision is
a) through studying your Bible.
b) trying new ideas of your own.
c) waiting for friends to tell you what to do.

4 There are many examples and suggestions in the Bible that give you principles to live by. As you study this course, pray that the Lord will give His wisdom to you and show you how to find and use these principles.

Check your answers.

Principle of Stewardship

Objective 3. *Define the principle of stewardship by following the guidelines for developing biblical principles.*

All that we have is from God. He created the world we live in. He upholds all things by His power. He sends seasons and harvests. So all the physical things that we have—houses, money, food—are His.

God created us, too, with our talents and intelligence. Not only did He create our life, but, through Jesus, He gives us eternal life. We are His children because He gave us that gift. All that we are is from God. It belongs to Him, too.

But God has given us a special privilege. He has given all things in Jesus Christ to us for His glory. Our possessions, our physical and mental abilities, and our time are only loaned to us. We are looking after them, making profitable use of them. God, who is the real owner, expects us to be wise. He will judge what we have done with what He has given to our care.

Remember the story Jesus told about the three servants? Their master went away leaving them with large sums of money. He had given them this money according to their ability. He expected them to use the money to buy and sell goods. Indeed two of the servants did that. They worked hard and earned a good profit for their master. But the third servant did nothing. He was not dishonest. He was afraid to use, and perhaps lose, what his master had given him. So he dug a hole and hid the money. When the master returned, he praised the servants who had worked hard. He gave them great rewards. But he was angry with the servant who had done nothing. He called him a bad and lazy servant, took away the money he had saved, and sent him away.

Two of the servants were "stewards." You will find that word used if you read this story in the King James Version (Matthew 25). Jesus told this story to show what God's Kingdom was like. As Christians we belong to God's Kingdom, and this story means something to us. It illustrates the principle of *stewardship*: the right use of what God has given to us to care for.

God Gives You Standards for Living

The Bible has much to say about stewardship. The Old Testament talks about *tithing*—giving one-tenth of all income and crops for God's work. It talks of giving the first fruits and the first born to God's service. The New Testament talks of sharing food and money with needy people, and giving for the gospel's sake. But joyfully giving back to God is only a *sign* of stewardship. By our giving we are aware that all we have is really the Lord's. It shows our attitude of willingness to do anything God wants.

Jesus stressed the importance of giving. His stories showed it, but He said it clearly:

> Much is required from the person to whom much is given (Luke 12:48).

Another illustration that Jesus used was *fruitfulness.* He told stories about plants that bore or did not bear fruit. It was of great concern to Him that God's children should be fruitful. He knew that Christians who used their abilities and resources for God would be fruitful. He knew that this would bring glory to God.

> My Father's glory is shown by your bearing much fruit; and in this way you become my disciples (John 15:8).

Fruitfulness comes from good stewardship. It is taking advantage of the special things God gives us. Being fruitful means using God's gifts for the good of others and for His glory. The apostle Peter urges us to be good managers (or stewards):

> Each one, as a good manager of God's different gifts, must use for the good of others the special gift he has received from God... so that in all things praise may be given to God through Jesus Christ (1 Peter 4:10-11).

The principle of stewardship in the life of the Christian is this: to be aware that God has given all things to be used wisely. Determine to use all of God's gifts to be a fruitful and responsible manager. He desires that we do everything for the good of others and the glory of God.

For You To Do

5 To which of the following areas can you apply the biblical principle of stewardship? Circle the letters of the appropriate answers.
  a) What do you do with your spare time
  b) How you perform your job each day
  c What color of clothes you wear
  d) How you spend the money you earn
  e) What and how you study

God Gives You Standards for Living

6 Think again about the decision you made and thought about for question 2. Was this something to which the principle of stewardship could apply? If not, can you think of a recent decision to which it could apply? Do you think you decided wisely?

Principle of Service

Objective 4. *Define the biblical principle of service by listing the ways it can affect your way of living.*

VERY IMPORTANT TO KNOW

Stewards are servants. Their job is to manage the things their master trusts them with. They have to understand that they are employed to follow orders. They must also know who it is that gives the orders: they must know their lord.

The Bible teaches that men have many kinds of masters. They are slaves to sin (Romans 6:20), to their fleshly desires (Ephesians 2:3, Romans 16:18), to the love of money (Matthew 6:24). The child of God has only one Lord and cannot serve two masters (Matthew 6:24). Our whole life must be given to the service of God.

This is a choice Christians must make, not once, but every day. Perhaps you remember the story of Joshua. He led the people of Israel into the Promised Land. With God's help, he drove out many nations. When Joshua was old he called his people together. He wanted to be sure they continued to serve God. He knew how easy it was for them to worship false gods and reminded them about the goodness of God. Then Joshua challenged them:

> Honor the Lord and serve him sincerely and faithfully. Get rid of the gods ... If you are not willing to serve him, decide today whom you will serve ... As for my family and me, we will serve the Lord (Joshua 24:14-15).

Joshua made his decision known: he would serve God till the day he died. He was a leader, but he was also a servant.

This was the attitude of our Lord Jesus, too. Though He had the nature of God, He did not use it to get His position. Instead, because He loved us and wanted to save us, He left all that He had in heaven. The Bible says that Jesus "took the nature of a servant" (Philippians 2:7). He became a man—not a powerful ruler giving orders for others to obey. Jesus was a servant, "He was humble and walked the path of obedience all the way to death—his death on the cross" (Philippians 2:8).

God Gives You Standards for Living

Jesus was a servant to God. He also served the people He came to save. In His life, He helped and healed and delivered. In His death, He set free from sin and hell. Jesus expected the same spirit of service in His disciples. One day they were quarreling over who would get important places when Jesus was king. Jesus told them that it was only unbelievers who wanted to have power and give orders. Then He gave them this principle of service:

> If one of you wants to be great, he must be the servant of the rest; and if one of you wants to be first, he must be your slave—like the Son of Man, who did not come to be served, but to serve and to give his life to redeem many people (Matthew 20:26-28).

The biblical principle of service is the opposite of the human principle of selfishness. It involves humility and willingness in service to God and other men. Listen to these directions:

> Love one another warmly as Christian brothers, and be eager to show respect for one another. Work hard and do not be lazy. Serve the Lord with a heart full of devotion (Romans 12:10-11).

> Submit yourselves to one another because of your reverence for Christ (Ephesians 5:21).

> Let love make you serve one another (Galatians 5:13).

Applying the principle of service is very difficult on a human level; we have to have help from God's Holy

Spirit. Through Him we are able to serve God and other people. Through Him we can obey and work and even suffer for Christ's sake. "The capacity we have comes from God" (2 Corinthians 3:5). In writing to men who were slaves, Paul gives us real encouragement to service:

> Whatever you do, work at it with all your heart, as though you were working for the Lord and not for men. Remember that the Lord will give you as a reward what he has kept for his people. For Christ is the real Master you serve (Colossians 3:23-24).

For You to Do

7 There are seven actions listed below. Circle the letters of those which illustrate the Principle of Service. Then rewrite the ones which are not circled and which illustrate the Principle of Selfishness so that they will show the Principle of Service. Your answers may not have the exact words ours do, but the idea should be the same.

1 **a** Taking a meal to someone who is sick
5 **b** Being too busy to help repair a friend's house
6 **c** Doing just enough work not to get dismissed
2 **d** Offering to help the pastor call on new Christians
7 **e** Insisting on being in charge at work
3 **f** Doing any job in the family that needs to be done
4 **g** Working even if no one gives you credit for the job

Check your answers.

God Gives You Standards for Living

APPLYING BIBLICAL PRINCIPLES

Objective 5. *Explain the practical nature of the principles studied by applying them to one example.*

Stewardship and service are only two of the many principles in the Bible. They are particularly important in the illustration we have used of the bicycle. But notice that the Law of love suggests many principles that we do not have time to study here: forgiveness (Ephesians 4:32), peace (1 Thessalonians 5:13), and joy (1 Thessalonians 5:16).

These principles are difficult to put into practice. If you rely on your own strength, you could not live according to them. But you are not alone, you have the Holy Spirit of God to strengthen you. Remember, you are a child of God and you are free to choose to do good. Remember Paul's words:

> Those who are led by God's Spirit are God's sons. For the Spirit that God has given you does not make you slaves and cause you to be afraid; instead, the Spirit makes you God's children (Romans 8:14-15).

Through the power of God's Spirit, you can apply God's principles to your daily problems. Making right decisions glorifies God and makes you a victorious Christian. That is God's will and command for you. Take John's words as an encouragement:

> For our love for God means that we obey his commands. And his commands are not too hard for us, because every child of God is able to defeat the world. And we win the victory over the world by means of our faith (1 John 5:3-4).

You can overcome your problems. No problem needs to be too hard for you to face. You are able to have complete victory through the love and power of God (Romans 8:37-39). God will give you wisdom to understand and apply His guidelines for action, using the principles in His Word. Each person must look at these principles and apply them.

> Put all things to the test: keep what is good and avoid every kind of evil (1 Thessalonians 5:21-22).

Again, let's use the idea of the new bicycle and the principle of stewardship. (We assume that riding a bicycle is possible where you live and that you know how to ride!)

1. Do you have the money to pay for it? Or, do you sincerely believe that God will provide the money? (Stewardship involves faith that God will provide as well as the responsible handling of finances.) Is this the best use for your money at this time? If you answered "yes," then maybe you may buy it.

2. If you use your money for this bicycle, will you be robbing God or others for whom you are responsible? Your answer is "no"? Then maybe you may buy it. Remember that not taking care of your family is the same as denying the faith (1 Timothy 5:8).

3. Do you *need* a bicycle? Can you find a good used bicycle for less money? With another bicycle, are you sure there would not be big repairs which cost time and money? If your answer to the first question is "yes," and a secondhand bicycle is not a possible or wise choice, then maybe you may buy it.

4. Do you spend much precious time walking, or repairing an old bicycle? Could your time be better spent if you had the convenience of a new bicycle? "Yes"? Then maybe you may buy it.

5. After prayer (and answering all these questions) are you convinced that God approves of your buying *this* new bicycle? If so, then you should buy it.

Notice we have stressed the positive side. God wants you to have the things which are best for you. Remember the command and promise of Jesus about our physical needs:

> Be concerned above everything else with the Kingdom of God and with what he requires of you, and he will provide you with all these other things (Matthew 6:33).

The condition is that we should be concerned with the things of God. Too often the desire or the possession of earthly goods leads to a lack of love for spiritual things. People with riches forget to depend on God's help. That was why God gave warnings to the people of Israel when they entered the Promised Land. If you have a Bible, read about this in (Deuteronomy 8:11-20).

This leads us to think about the principle we studied—service. We can apply this principle to the bicycle also. (In fact, many principles often have something to say about just one problem.)

1. Do you want a new bicycle in order to serve God better? Will it help you expand your work for Him? Are you sure it will not take time and energy away from God's work? "Yes" to these questions means that maybe you may buy it.

2. Are you sure that your desire for a new bicycle is not selfish? Are you sure it is not because you want praise or prestige or position? If the answer is still "yes," then maybe you may buy it.

3. Will having this new bicycle help you serve your family and church better? Are you sure it will not cause any division or quarreling? Will your family approve of your actions? "Yes" again? Then maybe you may buy it.

God Gives You Standards for Living

4. After prayer (and answering all these questions) are you convinced that it is God's will that you, His servant, have this bicycle? If so, then you should buy it.

Applying principles may sound like hard work. Sometimes it is. But when you arrive at a conclusion, you will have peace. You will know that you have followed the standards that God has given in His Word.

For You to Do

8 Smoking cigarettes is not mentioned in the Bible, but most Christians do not smoke. Can you think of some reasons why this is true?
  a Apply the principle of stewardship to this question and write your answer.
  b Now apply the principle of service and answer the question again.

Check your answer.

Check Your Answers

5 a What you do with your spare time.
  b How you perform your job each day.
  d How you spend the money you earn.
  e What and how you study.

1 b) reason you have for needing it and then pray before making your decision.

6 Your answer.

2 Your answer.

7 a Taking a meal to someone who is sick.
  d Offering to help the pastor call on new Christians.
  f Doing any job in the family that needs to be done.
  g Working even if no one gives you credit for the job.
  b Being willing to help repair a friend's house.
  c Doing your best at work.
  e Taking whatever job and authority is given you.

3 a) through studying your Bible.

8 Your answer may not be the same as ours, but you should have at least several of the same ideas:
  a) Stewardship
   1. This is not the *best* use of money.
   2. This is not a good way to use the body God has made. (Smoking is known to cause disease and to shorten life.)
   3. This is an activity that will continue to demand money. (Smoking is habit-forming.)
  b) Service
   Your answer.

4 Your answer.

Lesson 6: God Wants You to Care for Yourself

A car is a very complicated piece of machinery. Our knowledge of it is very limited. We understand more or less about how it works—the motor, the transmission, the steering, etc. We can wash and polish it. We can even change a flat tire. But we have never learned much about the mechanics of a car. What would we do if we ever had to do a major repair on our car?

We pray that day will never come, but if it did we know what we'd do first. We would get the maker's repair manual. In this book, the people who built our car explain how everything is put together. They tell us what to do to make our car run properly. Sometimes their instructions might seem strange to us, but we can trust their advice. After all, they were the people who designed and built our car. They ought to know what is best for it!

Human beings are much more complicated than a car. They like to think they know how to run their own life. But they barely understand the most obvious things about themselves—their mind, emotions, even bodily functions. The One who created all men does understand them. He has given instructions and advice

on how to live life properly. Sometimes people think that the Creator is unfair or strange in what He says. They find His instructions unreasonable and His advice old-fashioned. Yet isn't He the One who ought to know what is best?

As Christians, we have confidence that God knows what is good for us. We are also sure that, in all the ups and downs of life, He wants the very best for us. His rules and principles are for our benefit. They are to help us develop as whole and healthy persons, growing into the image of God. In this lesson, we will explore God's will for us as developing Christians. He wants us to be responsible and mature children of God.

In this lesson you will study ...

Four Ways God Expects You to Grow
Biblical Guidelines for Growth
    Guidelines for Your Body
    Guidelines for Your Mind
    Guidelines for Your Spirit
    Guidelines for Your Social Relationships

This lesson will help you ...

- Appreciate your responsibility for your growth as a person.
- Outline ways God expects you to grow.
- Identify biblical principles which will help you to grow.

FOUR WAYS GOD EXPECTS YOU TO GROW

Objective 1. *Give an example of the four areas of growth for the Christian developing into a whole person.*

The Bible tells us little about the youth and young manhood of Jesus. Yet that period is covered by these significant words: "Jesus grew both in body and in wisdom, gaining favor with God and man" (Luke 2:52).

The example of Jesus is important. He became mature by paying attention to four major areas of His personality: by exercise and work He grew physically strong (body); by study and thought He cultivated His

God Wants You to Care for Yourself

mind (wisdom); by prayer and hearing God's word He was spiritually alert (favor with God); by showing love and concern He became socially and emotionally acceptable (favor with man).

If He had neglected His physical development, He would not have been able to walk the roads of Palestine or stand the pain at Calvary. If He had not shown interest in others, He would not have been the friend of sinners or the close companion of His disciples. If He had not become intellectually capable, He would not have amazed all men with His understanding; even His enemies knew that nobody ever talked like He did (John 7:46). If he had neglected communion with His Heavenly Father, He would not have known God's perfect word and will.

But Jesus did all these things. He was the perfect man. He was whole in all things. He was holy. In many languages—including English—the word holiness comes from the word for wholeness or health. Jesus was a healthy, whole, and holy man, and Paul tells us to become like Him.

> We shall become mature people, reaching to the very height of Christ's full stature.... We must grow up in every way to Christ (Ephesians 4:13,15).

For You To Do

1. In your notebook write the passage from Ephesians 4 quoted above. Learn it and pray for God's help in making it true in your life.

2. Pray, asking God to show you how you are growing as a Christian. Then write in your notebook two short lists: one for the areas in which you see real progress; the other, for things where you have not changed much since becoming a Christian. Pray daily, using these lists, thanking God each time for ways you are becoming more like Jesus.

Check your answers with those given at the end of the lesson.

BIBLICAL GUIDELINES FOR GROWTH

Guidelines for Your Body

Objective 2. *List the ways which help or prevent the development of a healthy body.*

God gave us a marvelous body. He created it and it is good. Our body is the temple of the Holy Spirit. It is part of the body of Christ. "So," Paul urges us, "use your bodies for God's glory" (1 Corinthians 6:20). We do that by caring for our bodies. Here are the principles of stewardship and service again. As the apostle says a little earlier, "The body is not to be used for sexual immorality, but to serve the Lord; and the Lord provides for the body" (1 Corinthians 6:13).

God has created our body with needs. But He has provided for those needs. For example, marriage is God's provision for the sexual needs of male and female. Paul advises those whom God has not called to a single life to marry and to satisfy their partner's sexual needs.

Sexual immorality and perversion are equally displeasing to God. They are sins *against* our body (1 Corinthians 6:18), that God wants to be holy and useful for His service.

The same principle of respect for our body applies to eating and drinking. The Lord Jesus fasted and prayed. But He also enjoyed good meals with His friends (though His enemies condemned Him for it). Romans

14 tells us that there is no special goodness in eating or not eating particuar foods.

> God's Kingdom is not a matter of eating and drinking, but of the righteousness, peace, and joy which the Holy Spirit gives (Romans 14:17).

With these important guidelines in mind, the mature Christian *chooses* what to eat and drink. He is mindful that excess is sin, for it abuses his body. That is why Paul warned against drunkenness and over-eating. For example he advised us: "Do not get drunk with wine, which will only ruin you; instead, be filled with the Spirit" (Ephesians 5:18).

We glorify God by keeping our bodies under control. A body *out of control* through abuse of alcohol or drugs, tobacco or marijuana, is displeasing to God.

Respect for our body as God's temple is shown in the fruit of the Spirit called self-control. By the Holy Spirit's help, we can determine to keep our bodies holy and clean for God's Spirit to live in.

A healthy body is a useful body. It can work, and work is part of God's plan. Jesus was always busy doing good things. When men criticized Him, He told them that He was acting like His Heavenly Father: "My Father is always working, and I too must work" (John 5:17). Physical work is good for you. It is a good use of your body. Perhaps your job does not let you use your muscles. Then you must take time to exercise your body. "Physical exercise has some value" (1 Timothy 4:8) wrote Paul who sometimes used athletes and boxers as examples of discipline. Running, walking, bicycling, working in a garden—these are good for the person whose job is mostly at a desk. Listen to Paul again:

> "Work hard and do not be lazy. Serve the Lord with a heart full of devotion" (Romans 12:11).

But God is not a slave-driver. Remember, he always has our best interests at heart. He knows that work alone would kill us, one way or another. For a weary body there is *rest*. There has to be rest, or there is breakdown. God made rest a part of His creation. The night was made for sleep. The seventh day is the day of rest and re-creation.

Pastors and Christian workers who work so hard on Sundays need to be reminded: God requires a day of rest. Jesus Himself needed quiet and relaxation. So did His disciples. One time there were so many people coming to Jesus, that they did not even have time to eat. So Jesus said, "Let us go off by ourselves to some place where we will be alone and you can rest a while" (Mark 6:31).

Remember the concern Jesus showed for the tired and hungry crowds. Service to Jesus brings times of refreshing. Jesus calls to all His workers:

> Come to me, all of you who are tired from carrying heavy loads, and I will give you rest. Take my yoke and put it on you ... and you will find rest (Matthew 11:28-29).

For You To Do

3 Circle the letter before each statement below that tells you how to have a strong and healthy body.
  a Do hard physical work.
  b Keep God's laws on sexual morality.
  c Stay in bed all day.
  d Eat as often and as much as you can.
  e Have times of exercise and rest.
  f Use your wages to get drunk.
  g Eat regularly and wisely.

4 Write this important scriptural direction in your notebook. Learn it and find at least three ways each day to apply it to your life: "You do not belong to yourselves but to God; he bought you for a price. So use your bodies for God's glory" (1 Corinthians 6:19-20).

Check your answers.

Guidelines for Your Mind

Objective 3. *Describe ways the Christian can develop his mind and talents and acquire wisdom.*

It's obvious that all work, and all service to God too, is not physical. We serve God and men by using our minds. Brain work can be hard work! Learning is wonderful exercise!

Imagine that you had a child with a lazy mind. He was of normal intelligence, but didn't want to learn. He wouldn't listen when you talked with him. He refused to

God Wants You to Care for Yourself 109

learn to talk himself. Instead of going to school with other children, he just sat there. Would you be happy with that child? Of course not. If the child were sick, or mentally not normal, then you would understand. God would give you love and pity and patience. But if the child was willfully ignorant and inactive, then you would be right to be upset.

There are many children of God who are mentally lazy. You are not because you are working hard on this course. But there are many. They accept Jesus as Savior. Perhaps they go to church. But, like the steward who did not use his money, they do nothing with the riches God has given them. They never learn to hear God's voice; they never learn to speak to Him in prayer; they never study God's Word for themselves; they believe everything anybody tells them (even wrong teaching about God); they just sit there.

Do you know people like that? If so, you need to help them. You are strong and they are weak. You are to "build them up in the faith" (Romans 15:1-2). Teach them these lessons on how a Christian grows mature in wisdom:

1. Teach them to read so that they can read the Bible and good literature. Do not say, "The government school should teach them to read." It is a work for the church, particularly with older people.
2. Help them learn to pray. It is not great words that matter, but needs and thanks simply shared with God our Father (Philippians 4:6).

3. Help them with Bible study. First they need to gain knowledge of God's ways—the facts about Jesus and His kingdom. Then they need to know how to apply the knowledge, for that is wisdom.

By studying and practicing God's ways, you will grow wiser. The Psalmist asked himself how to be happy and have a pure life. He answered himself, saying that it was in using his mind to study the ways of the Lord.

> I study your instructions: I examine your teachings. I take pleasure in your laws; your commands I will not forget (Psalm 119:15-16).

Now the Psalmist was a poet and a thinker. He was able to put God-inspired thoughts into beautiful language. He had a gift from God for using words. He

God Wants You to Care for Yourself   111

had worked at developing that gift. He understood the art of making poems that his own people would love.

That is one aspect of the *creative* side of man's mind. God is creative. He has made us creative like Him. Christians, who want to be like their Father the Creator, should shine in creativity, in their job and in their pastimes. When Moses was making the Sacred Tent, God gave him special helpers. They were skilled craftsmen and artists. About one of them the Bible says:

> God has filled him with his power (or Spirit) and given him skill, ability, and understanding for every kind of artistic work (Exodus 35:31).

Ability to tell stories, speak well, make poems, sing songs, paint pictures, make designs, sculpt wood or stone, make and act out plays, explain Scripture simply and correctly, see work that needs to be done and know how to do it—all this is a gift of God's Spirit. And we are given gifts to use and to develop for God's glory and the good of the church.

What gifts do you have? Do you know the songs and poems of your people? Study more and ask God's help to create *good* songs and poems. Can you play a musical instrument? Practice hard. Good playing glorifies God. Perhaps it is time you studied how to create new music in your culture. The church in your country needs songs which speak to your people in the music and poetry they understand. Remember what Peter said about stewardship:

Each one, as a good manager of God's different gifts, must use for the good of others the special gift he has received from God (1 Peter 4:10).

For You To Do

5 Circle the letter before the ways you can develop your mind and wisdom.
   a Always believe everything people tell you.
   b Study the Word of God.
   c Read good books.
   d Never ask questions.
   e Take ICI courses.
   f Listen to older Christians.
   g Refuse to discuss what you believe.

6 Set aside a special time of prayer each day this week to think and pray about the special gift or gifts you have received from God. Write in your notebook any gifts you think you have, and then write briefly how you are going to use them for the good of others.

Check your answers.

Guidelines for Your Spirit

Objective 4. *Identify spiritual growth as increasing awareness of God's ways and putting them into action.*

Objective 5. *List three methods given in scripture by which spiritual growth is possible.*

God Wants You to Care for Yourself

When Jesus was a child, "the favor of God was upon him" (Luke 2:40). God was pleased with Him as He grew to manhood. At His baptism the voice from heaven said: "You are my own dear Son. I am pleased with you" (Luke 3:22). Not only had Jesus grown in human wisdom and strength so that He was a man, He had also grown in understanding God's ways. He knew that He was God's Son; He had learned what God wanted Him to do; He was ready in all things to do what God told Him. This was pleasing to God.

When His enemies questioned who He was, Jesus told them that they would find out one day. He added:

> When you lift up the Son of Man, you will know that "I Am Who I Am"; then you will know that I do nothing on my own authority, but I say only what the Father has instructed me to say. And he who sent me is with me; he has not left me alone, because I always do what pleases him (John 8:28-29).

Jesus said and did nothing that did not come from God's command to Him. That is why He was always sure of God's presence and approval in each word or action. He learned and acted on God's will even when that was difficult. Remember His prayer in Gethsemane: "Not what I want, but what you want" (Matthew 26:39).

Growing in God's favor comes from learning to say that prayer sincerely. It is finding out God's ways (those rules and principles) for all His children, and putting them into practice. It is discovering God's special will for your life and acting on it.

In Lesson 3 you studied four methods God uses to help us know what He wants us to become. Do you remember them? A purified conscience; the Word of God; the examples of Jesus; the Holy Spirit's guidance. These work together as we seek God's will out of our desire to please Him.

With a pure conscience, asking the Holy Spirit to guide, study the Word of God, and in it the teaching and life of the Savior. Personal Bible reading is essential for Christian growth.

The Jews of Berea, to whom Paul preached about Jesus, are a good example to us.

> They listened to the message with great eagerness, and every day they studied the Scriptures to see if what Paul said was really true. Many of them believed (Acts 17:11-12).

God Wants You to Care for Yourself 115

Notice how these sincere people read: they thoughtfully, "every day" continually, "to see" purposefully, and "believed" willingly. For spiritual growth, a Christian too must study God's Word daily, seek God's will, and prepare to put it into action.

In addition to personal Bible study, the Christian has another gift of God to help him: pastors and teachers. These men, from their study and experience, share with other believers the insights given them in God's Word. They bring God's message to build up His people (see Ephesians 4:11-16).

Those who became Christians on the day of Pentecost learned that they needed instruction from those older in the faith.

> They spent their time in learning from the apostles, taking part in the fellowship, and sharing in the fellowship meals and the prayers (Acts 2:42).

These Christians learned from the apostles who had been taught by Jesus and were filled with the Holy Spirit. Christians today need teachers and pastors who know God's Word and are Spirit-filled. The Bible teaches that we are to obey and submit to such leaders (Hebrews 13:17) and to be grateful for their teaching (Galatians 6:6).

But it is not just the pastors who teach in a local church. Because the church is the body of believers, encouragement and witness should come from all the members. By our lives and words, we can teach each other. The apostle Paul gives us this exhortation:

Christ's message in all its richness must live in your hearts. Teach and instruct one another with all wisdom (Colossians 3:16).

When Christians come together, there can be sharing of knowledge about God's ways. A striking biblical example of this concerns the gifted preacher Apollos. Though he knew the Scriptures and the facts about Jesus, it seems that he was not filled with the Spirit. So Aquila and Priscilla "took him home with them and explained to him more correctly the Way of God" (Acts 18:26). The ministry of Apollos was transformed by this act of sharing.

It is important to see, too, the humility of Apollos. He had a teachable spirit. He accepted instruction from others, though he was an important and eloquent preacher. We will not learn from God's Word nor from others if we resist their teaching. We must be prepared to obey. We must sincerely desire to follow God's ways.

God Wants You to Care for Yourself

Remember the illustration of the repair manual with which this lesson began? How foolish if I read what it said and then refused to obey! Just so with God's Word. To please God, to grow in his favor, you have to do everything His way, just as our Lord Jesus did. However much we have grown by living for God, the Bible tells us there is still room for growth:

> You learned from us how you should live in order to please God. This is, of course, the way you have been living. And now we beg and urge you in the name of the Lord Jesus to do even more (1 Thessalonians 4:1).

For You To Do

7 Circle the letter which corresponds with every activity that helps the Christian grow in favor with God.
- **a)** Praying for the Spirit's guidance
- **b)** Studying the Scriptures for yourself
- **c** Listening to complaining
- **d** Reading the Bible while thinking about something else
- **e)** Learning from other Christians' experience
- **f** Questioning God's rules and principles
- **g)** Daily reading of God's Word
- **h)** Paying attention to good teaching

8 If you do not already study the Bible regularly and systematically, determine to begin right away. Write in your notebook a time each day you will give some minutes to serious, prayerful reading. Write down the books you intend to read first: many Christians are helped by reading and thinking about short passages from the New Testament, the Psalms, and the Old Testament, every day. Ask an older Christian or pastor for his advice.

Check your answers.

Guidelines for Your Social Relationships

Objective 6. *Explain the importance of acting with wisdom and respect towards non-Christians.*

Jesus was a man people liked. Mothers brought their children for Him to place His hands on them (Mark 10:13). Men left their homes and jobs to follow Him during His ministry. Though He had many enemies, it was not because He was harsh or cruel or proud or wicked. It was because they "rejected God's purpose for themselves" (Luke 7:30) and despised Him as "a friend of tax collectors and other outcasts" (Luke 7:34).

The first Christians were like their Master. They cared about the sick and poor. They ate together "with glad and humble hearts, praising God, and enjoying the good will (or favor) of all the people" (Acts 2:46-47).

Can we live in such a way that we please both men and God? The apostle Paul seems to make these opposites:

God Wants You to Care for Yourself

Does this sound as if I am trying to win man's approval? No indeed! What I want is God's approval! Am I trying to be popular with men? If I were still trying to do so, I would not be a servant of Christ (Galatians 1:10).

But here he is talking about adapting his teaching—the unchanging gospel of Christ—to the desires of sinful men. That we Christians cannot do. We cannot change our beliefs nor our righteous behavior to please other people. No! We must serve God first. It is for God's sake that we obey the laws of men, as the apostle Peter tells us.

> "For God wants you to silence the ignorant talk of foolish people by the good things you do" (1 Peter 2:15).

We are witnesses to other people by our good deeds. Paul was happy to commend the Christians of Thessalonica for their brotherly love. He encourages them to do even more:

> Make it your aim to live a quiet life, to mind your own business, and to earn your own living, just as we told you before. In this way you will win the respect of those who are not believers, and you will not have to depend on anyone for what you need (1 Thessalonians 4:11-12).

We grow in favor with other men as we work quietly and well, for then we are neither a problem nor a burden. Moreover, we are to show concern by our behavior towards other people. Paul wanted Christians to be wise in their conduct towards those who were not believers, and in discussions to be always pleasant and interesting (Colossians 4:5-6). He instructs Titus to remind his people to be submissive and ready to do good, and gives good advice:

> Tell them not to speak evil of anyone, but to be peaceful and friendly, and always to show a gentle attitude towards everyone (Titus 3:2).

Paul contrasts our lives now with our lives before we became God's children; then, he says, "others hated us and we hated them" (Titus 3:3). As we show our love to others by our respect and gentleness, we will not always win them for Christ. But many will recognize our concern and not find in our behavior an excuse to criticize the gospel. The proof of our good actions is not whether all people say good things about us now, but whether they must recognize our goodness before God Himself.

God Wants You to Care for Yourself

Your conduct among the heathen should be so good that when they accuse you of being evildoers, they will have to recognize your good deeds, and so praise God on the Day of his coming (1 Peter 2:12).

For You To Do

9 Write 1 Thessalonians 4:11-12 in your notebook and memorize it. Pray about the specific ways you can apply this verse to your own life.

10 List several reasons why it is important to use wisdom and respect with the people around you who are not Christians.
To be a good witness
To grow in favor of men because of love
To show your own concern by your behavior

Check Your Answers

6 Your answer.

1 Your answer.

7 a) Praying for the Spirit's guidance.
   b) Studying the Scriptures for yourself.
   e) Learning from other Christians' experiences.
   g) Daily reading of God's Word.
   h) Paying attention to good teaching.

2 Your answer.

8 Your answer.

3 **a** True.
   b True.
   c False.
   d False.
   e True.
   f False.
   g True.

9 Your answer.

4 Your answer.

10 To be a good witness.
   To grow in favor with men because of love.
   To show our concern by our behavior.

5 b) Study the Word of God.
   c) Read good books.
   e) Take ICI courses.
   f) Listen to older Christians.

Lesson 7: God Wants You to Care for the Church

The church is the body of Christ with Jesus Himself the head. We Christians are members or parts of the body. The apostle Paul develops this idea in 1 Corinthians 12. He shows how important each part is to the whole, how each part is concerned for the others, and how all parts suffer or are content together.

I experienced this after I had been outside playing football with my son. When I sat down to work, I noticed that my feet were hot and tired. It seemed that all I could think of was my hot tired feet. So my hands took care of my feet. I took off my shoes and I washed my feet. My feet were then cool and rested, and my whole body relaxed. I could work again.

Another picture of the church is the family. Perhaps you would like to review Lesson 1 before beginning the new material in this lesson. We saw there that we are sons and daughters in God's family.

Members of a family need each other, take care of each other, and can meet each other's needs. They work and play together, mourn and rejoice together. They share food, beds, money, problems—even sicknesses. Sometimes, unfortunately, they fight among themselves even though, deep down, they really love each other. Most often they are united in love, ready to defend each other against the whole world.

The law of love is of greatest importance in the family of God, or the body of Christ. In this lesson we will see how the law of love is applied through the principles of service and stewardship in the church.

In this lesson you will study ...

Unity in the Family of God
Service in the Family of God
Stewardship in the Family of God

This lesson will help you ...

- Explain the importance of unity in the family of God.
- Give examples of ways you can serve the body of Christ in love.
- Identify ways of being a wise steward of your possessions and gifts for the good of the church.

UNITY IN THE FAMILY OF GOD

Objective 1. *Describe the importance of unity in the body of Christ.*

Objective 2. *Identify some causes of disunity and ways to overcome them.*

Before Jesus gave Himself on the cross, He prayed for those who would believe and become part of His church. His prayer was simple, but profound:

"I pray that they may all be one" (John 17:21).

Unity is vital to the spiritual development of the church. Sometimes there is disunity in a person's body. A group of cells reject the control of the rest of the body; they grow rapidly and end up killing the person.

God Wants You to Care for the Church 127

It is the dreaded disease of cancer. In a church, disunity can also kill.

This was what concerned Paul about the church in Corinth. The Corinthians did not recognize the singleness of Christ's body, and were in danger of destroying it. What they needed was *love* to heal their divisions (1 Corinthians 13).

The book of James deals with another problem of disunity in his epistle: prejudice. He was upset to see that believers were being treated differently according to what they looked like (James 2:9). He found this kind of distinction evil and foolish. It is against the law of love:

> You will be doing the right thing if you obey the law of the Kingdom, which is found in the scripture, 'Love your neighbor as you love yourself.' But if you treat people according to their outward appearance, you are guilty of sin (James 2:8-9).

Christians must not make distinctions based on riches, education or race. Because your brother is poor, or cannot read, or has a different shaped nose, does that make him any less your brother? The same is true in the family of God.

Indeed, in God's family all the principles of the world are rejected. Paul said that the man who thought he was "wise by this world's standards . . . . should become a fool, in order to be really wise" (1 Corinthians 3:18). Jesus told his quarreling disciples: "If one of you wants to be great, he must be the servant of the rest"

(Matthew 20:26). He also said: "Whoever tries to gain his own life will lose it; but whoever loses his life for my sake will gain it" (Matthew 10:39).

There is sadness in a father's heart when one child thinks he is superior to all the others. Since we enter God's family by grace, there is no place for boasting (Ephesians 2:9). There is sadness too when a child wants everything for himself and will not share or work with the others. The Father does not want selfish or lazy children, either. Boasting, selfishness, laziness— these are worldly principles. In the church, the principles of humble service and loving stewardship should be put into action, so that there might be unity.

Your life in Christ makes you strong, and his love comforts you. You have fellowship with the Spirit, and you have kindness and compassion for one another. I urge you, then, to make me completely happy by having the same thoughts, sharing the same love, and being one in soul and mind. Don't do anything from selfish ambition or from a cheap desire to boast, but be humble towards one another, always considering others better than yourselves. And look out for one another's interests, not just for your own (Philippians 2:1-4).

For You To Do

1 Write Philippians 2:1-4 in your notebook. Draw a circle around the words which are Christian qualities and draw a line through the words which are worldly ones. Consider prayerfully where you are in relation to both of these qualities. Can you find a way to put into practice these Christian qualities this week?

SERVICE IN THE FAMILY OF GOD

Objective 3. *Describe ways that the law of love can be made practical through service.*

As part of Christ's body, members of God's family, we are instructed to live, work, and worship in harmony. Since we are not yet perfect, there are sometimes problems in the church. Disunity creeps in all too easily. We need only read Acts to see that—or Corinthians, or Philippians 4:2. The Bible does not hide how difficult people find it to leave behind the world's standards.

Frequently, believers are urged to love each other, not in theory but in reality:

> Love must be completely sincere.... Love one another warmly as Christian brothers, and be eager to show respect for one another (Romans 12:9-10).

Respect is one way to show love. Too often young people, who have more schooling, fail to respect older Christians. This is wrong, as well as foolish (see 1 Timothy 5:1). On the other hand, Paul encouraged Timothy to expect respect from older people, though he was young (1 Timothy 4:12).

Respect is an attitude. Love must express itself also in action: doing good to our Christian brothers.

> So let us not become tired of doing good .... as often as we have the chance, we should do good to everyone, and especially to those who belong to our family in the faith (Galatians 6:9-10).

How can we do good? First we must keep at heart the interests of our brothers, not just our own (1 Corinthians 10:24). This is particularly necessary when they are new or weak Christians. We must avoid doing things to harm their faith. More than that, we must help them even when it is inconvenient or displeasing to us.

> We who are strong in the faith ought to help the weak to carry their burdens. We should not please ourselves. Instead, we should all please our brothers for their own good, in order to build them up in the faith (Romans 15:1-2).

God Wants You to Care for the Church

Paul goes on to tell us in this passage that dealing with other people requires the patience (verse 5) and acceptance or tolerance (verse 7) which Christ showed in his "life of service" (verse 8).

To do good we must also be aware of people's needs. Is someone in the church sick, out of work, or in need of food? It is our job as loving brothers to notice and, if we can, to help.

> Keep on loving one another as Christian brothers. Remember to welcome strangers in your homes. There were some who did that and welcomed angels without knowing it. Remember those who are in prison, as though you were in prison with them. Remember those who are suffering, as though you were suffering as they are (Hebrews 13:1-3).

Here the general commandment to love is followed by exact directions. Remember to be hospitable; remember to visit the prisoners; remember to help the suffering. Jesus said that, at the final judgment, men would be judged by whether they did this kind of thing or not. Showing pity in a practical way to a brother is a way of showing love for the Lord.

> Whenever you did this for one of the least important of these brothers of mine, you did it for me! (Matthew 25:40).

Some people, busy with religious activities, sometimes forget that faith must be put into practice. This is the message of James, when he describes genuine religion: "to take care of orphans and widows in their suffering and to keep oneself from being corrupted by the world" (James 1:27).

It was a religion of loving unity and practical compassion which marked the first believers. When they knew of a need, they acted, just as Jesus always did, from compassion and love. This should be a goal for our life in the family of God as well.

> The group of believers was one in mind and heart. No one said that any of his belongings was his own, but they all shared with one another everything they had (Acts 4:32).

God Wants You to Care for the Church

For You To Do

2 Circle the letter before each TRUE statement below that shows an expression of service to the body of Christ.
   a Criticize the pastor for his lack of love.
   b Cultivate the garden of a sick widow.
   c Help a new Christian learn to read a portion of the Bible.
   d Help the family of a Christian in prison for his faith.
   e Laugh at a brother with ragged clothes.
   f Invite an unimportant church visitor to your house.
   g Help a rich Christian in hope of getting a job from him.

3 In Lesson 1 we asked you to think about the Christian brothers in your community and their needs. We asked you if you were part of God's answer to those needs. By now you should be able to see more quickly their problems and be more ready to help. In your notebook list five people in your Christian family whom you can help and write what you did.

STEWARDSHIP IN THE FAMILY OF GOD

Objective 4. *Describe several ways that the law of love can be made practical through stewardship.*

The first believers, who showed their love and unity by sharing their possessions, were serving each other. They were also using their belongings in a way showing responsible stewardship. This sharing of wealth is found throughout the New Testament. When the Christians at Antioch knew there was to be a famine, they "decided that each of them would send as much as he could to help their fellow-believers who lived in Judea" (Acts 11:29). Perhaps Paul remembered that incident when he wrote to the church at Rome:

> "Share your belongings with your needy fellow-Christians, and open your homes to strangers" (Romans 12:13).

Hospitality, like sharing, is both service and stewardship. It helps others, and it is the wise and proper use of the homes which God has allowed us to have. Remember what was said about stewardship in Lesson 5—all our possessions are loaned to us to be used rightly, for the good of others and for God's glory. That includes giving for the work of the gospel, both locally and in missionary activity. The apostle John commended his friend Gaius for his faithful giving to Christian workers, even strangers to him. John gave a good reason for sharing this way:

> We Christians, then, must help these people, so that we may share in their work for the truth (3 John 8).

By supporting those who work for God, we are taking part in the work they do, we are involved in their ministry. Besides, such giving is "like a sweet-smelling offering to God, a sacrifice which is acceptable and pleasing to him" (Philippians 4:18).

We can also be involved in the ministry of the church in a personal way. Perhaps you already give time and energy to spreading the gospel in your area and helping the believers in your church. That is wonderful! God desires us to do our best to work for Him. But perhaps you need some guidance on how you may best serve the church and be a wise steward of God's gifts to you.

This was the case in the Corinthian church in regard to spiritual gifts. These believers were eager, but without knowledge. They thought everyone should show the same spiritual ability or gift. Paul reminded them that they were the body of Christ, and that bodies have different parts for different functions. He listed several gifts of the Spirit, and begged the Corinthians to use spiritual gifts in love and to help the church (1 Corinthians 14:1, 4).

The purpose of all God's gifts is to build up the church, that is, to help the Christians to learn to be more like Jesus (1 Corinthians 14:12). Some of these gifts are for use in church services, to worship God and proclaim His message, yet they are always to build up the church (1 Corinthians 14:26). Others are less noticeable, but just as necessary: serving, teaching, sharing, organizing, showing kindness (Romans 12:6-8).

Now, we Christians are parts of Christ's body and each part has a different job (Romans 12:4-5).

> "So we are to use our different gifts in accordance with the grace that God has given us" (Romans 12:6).

As stewards of God's gracious gifts, we have to do three things. First, we must search our lives, pray to God, and ask mature Christians about the gifts we may have. Second, we must use and develop the gifts we know we have—for the building up of the church—while praying for other gifts and for love (1 Corinthians 12:31). Third, we must encourage other Christians to do the same: that way, we help them to be good stewards too, just as Barnabas helped Saul, and later the apostle Paul, to develop his great gift of teaching (see Acts 11:25-26).

Remember that it is the Lord Jesus Himself who gives gifts to us—whether they are natural abilities or spiritual gifts of the Spirit. As Ephesians 4:7-16 teaches us, He gives them to prepare all of His people to serve Him better and to build up the whole church. To function correctly within the church then, to be good stewards of His gifts, we must aim at growing mature under His direction.

> Under his control all the different parts of the body fit together, and the whole body is held together by every joint with which it is provided. So when each

separate part works as it should, the whole body grows and builds itself up through love (Ephesians 4:16).

For You To Do

4 Circle the letter before each activity below which shows good stewardship toward the body of Christ.
a Sharing a hymn God has given you.
b Bringing visiting Christians into your home.
c Being ready for God to use you to build up the church.
d Trying to be the only one to pray or speak in tongues in church.
e Supporting others' ministries by gifts and prayers.
f Allowing others to share their insights into Scripture.

5 Pray, either alone or with a mature Christian, about what gifts God has given you. In your notebook, write down at least one gift you think you have received and ways in which you can help the body by using it. You may want to ask your pastor or another Christian to give you guidance about when and how you can best develop your gift.

Check Your Answers

3 Your answer.

1 Words to circle: Kindness, compassion, having the same thoughts, sharing the same love, being one in soul and mind, be humble, considering others better than yourself, look out for one another's interest.
Words to draw line through: selfish ambition, cheap desire to boast, just for your own (interests).

4 a Sharing a hymn God has given you.
  b Bringing visiting Christians into your home.
  c Being ready for God to use you to build up the church.
  d Supporting others' ministries by gifts and prayers.
  e Allowing others to share their insights into Scripture.

2 a False.
  b True.
  c True.
  d True.
  e False.
  f True.
  g False.

5 Your answer.

Lesson 8

God Sent You to Care for the World

What would you do if you owed a friend more money than you could pay? In the region of Africa where we lived, there was a simple way. A bag of salt was sufficient to cancel all debts. Of course, this custom came from a time when salt was hard to find. Everybody needed salt and if you could obtain it, you were very happy.

Salt is an important part of life. It is used to preserve foods. It can be used to clean wounds (though that hurts!) and heal sore throats. And, because of its flavor we use salt to make our meals taste better.

Jesus said: "Salt is good" (Luke 14:34). He also said that those who believed in Him were like salt: "You are like salt for all mankind" (Matthew 5:13). And He warned His disciples against losing their *saltiness*.

What does this illustration mean? Jesus was saying first that His people had to *be different*. Just as men recognize salt by its taste, so everyone should know Christians by their special way of living. Secondly, Jesus implied that Christians have a job to do in the world. We are to have a preserving and purifying influence on society.

140

The world needs our saltiness, our light, and our message. We must be, do, and say all that God commands. Our purpose in life is to represent the grace and justice of God to the world, so that the world will know and be saved.

In This Lesson You Will Study...

Salt Preserves: Showing the Love of God
Salt Purifies: Showing the Righteousness of God
Salt Flavors: Spreading the Message of God

This Lesson Will Help You...

- Describe the influence that your Christian life should have on the world.

- Discover the kinds of service God has for you to do in your community.

SALT PRESERVES:
SHOWING THE LOVE OF GOD

Objective 1. *Determine specific ways to show how love to your neighbor can be expressed.*

> Dear friends, let us love one another, because love comes from God. Whoever loves is a child of God and knows God. Whoever does not love does not know God, for God is love (1 John 4:7-8).

There is no doubt that the first evidence of being God's child is having love. In the last lesson we saw the importance of loving our Christian brothers. It fostered unity, inspired good deeds, and built up the church.

Real Christian love—which is not just talk but action (1 John 3:18)—has a still wider impact. Jesus knew this when He commanded His disciples to love one another, just as He loved them:

> "If you have love for one another, then everyone will know that you are my disciples" (John 13:35).

We know that love is necessary to preserve life, yet the world in which we live is deprived of real love. When people see men and women who are genuinely concerned for each other's welfare, they are surprised. One church leader said that if Christians today really showed love as the Bible commands, people would be crowding to the doors of our churches. And a Christian writer has stated that the church should function as a life-saving station which provides the love which the world needs. Indeed Jesus implied that other

God Sent You to Care for the World 143

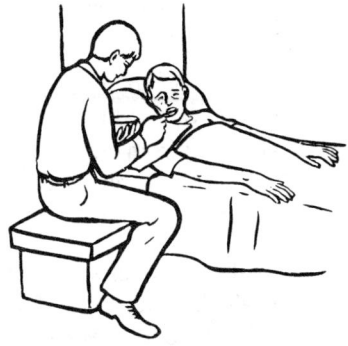

people would be convinced by the love which they saw between Christians who were united in love. He prayed:

> I pray that they may all be one. Father! May they be in us, just as you are in me and I am in you. May they be one, so that the world will believe that you sent me (John 17:21).

The love which God has put in our hearts is not just for other Christians. God loves all the world, and we are called to love the people of the whole world too. Our love is salt for them. Paul encourages believers who were known for their brotherly love:

> "May the Lord make your love for one another and for all people grow more and more" (1 Thessalonians 3:12).

The great commandments of God were to love God Himself, and to love our neighbor as ourself. When a lawyer asked Jesus who his neighbor was, Jesus told the parable of the Good Samaritan. This story tells us both that the persons we are to love may be anyone we meet, and that our love must be *in deed*.

How can we express love to our neighbors? As with our Christian brothers, we need to care and share. We do not set ourselves apart from other men as though we do not have problems. It is simply that we know God is with us, and so we can relate to others in their distress:

> He helps us in all our troubles, so that we are able to help others who have all kinds of troubles, using the same help that we ourselves have received from God (2 Corinthians 1:4).

Jesus Himself knew what hunger was like. So when He saw the hungry crowds, He was sorry for them. He fed them with the multiplied loaves and fishes (Matthew 15:32-38). We need to feed the hungry of our world, and help them learn to provide food for themseles.

Because we are just forgiven sinners, we should know not to set ourselves apart from others for reasons of prejudice or self-righteousness. Jesus was called the friend of sinners. When He showed love by visiting Zaccheus, He did not condemn him. But soon Zaccheus was a changed man—because Jesus made Himself available to him.

> "For God did not send his Son into the world to be its judge, but to be its savior" (John 3:17).

As a Christian you also have been similarly sent into the world by Christ to help the poor, sick, distressed, and needy, to seek and to save the lost (John 17:18).

For You To Do

1. Write 1 Thessalonians 3:12 in your notebook and memorize it. Make this a daily prayer for yourself.

2. After praying the prayer above, look about you in your community or job. Are there people you know with problems? Does someone need friendship, food, clothes, or some other kind of help? Make a list of these people and see what you can do to be the salt in their situation.

SALT PURIFIES: SHOWING THE RIGHTEOUSNESS OF GOD

Objective 2. *Name some ways in which your life can reflect God's righteousness in your community.*

The world we live in is filled with injustice and wrong. Consequently the people of the world do not understand the righteousness of God. The children of God are in the world to continue the work of Jesus, and to make God's goodness known. By this means, they bring in a purifying influence into society: they are salt.

We saw earlier that most people's attitudes and actions result from motives of selfishness, pride, laziness, or a desire for money, pleasure, or popularity. Those were our motives too, before Christ saved us and we became God's children. Now we are to have better motives and more holy actions. This will mean changing what we are doing.

> The man who used to rob must stop robbing and start working, in order to earn an honest living for himself and to be able to help the poor. Do not use harmful words, but only helpful words, the kind that build up and provide what is needed, so that what you say will do good to those who hear you (Ephesians 4:28-29).

In our personal lives we should demonstrate the fruit of the Spirit (Galatians 5:22). Our conduct should be recognizably different from other people's (1 Peter 2:12). We should be honest, hard-working, and just.

Moreover we should try to see that honesty, hard work, and justice prevail in our community. When Jesus saw that evil merchants were robbing the worshipers in the temple, he was angry and drove them out (Matthew 21:12-13). Jesus was concerned with what was fair and right; he hated hypocrisy and lying in all things.

For this reason He opposed the unfairness of the Pharisees. He called these apparently religious men "whitewashed tombs": they tried to look good on the outside, but inside—as people well knew—they were really "full of hypocrisy and sins" (Matthew 23:27-28).

God acts against those who cheat and lie. He did not allow the deception of Ananias and Sapphira to go unpunished (Acts 5:1-11). They tried to lie about how much of their money they were giving to God. But the Holy Spirit told Peter, and God struck them dead. Their lie was a mockery of His power and a dishonor to the church.

God is not slow to judge the enemies of Christ, through the words of His servants. Think of Elymas the magician, who opposed Paul and Barnabas (see Acts 13:6-12). He tried to stop the gospel with all kinds of evil; he tried to turn the truth about Jesus into lies. But God punished him with blindness.

Now God does not always act directly as He did in those examples, but He expects us to do what we can to correct wrong actions. Our holy God hates all injustices. The Old Testament is very clear about this. For example God had often to reprimand His people for their failure to maintain the rights of the poor in their community.

> See that justice is done—help those who are oppressed, give orphans their rights, and defend widows (Isaiah 1:17).

Again and again God spoke to His people about the same social problems which trouble all people. He gave clear instructions:

> These are the things you should do: Speak the truth to one another. In the courts give real justice—the kind that brings peace. Do not plan ways of harming one another. Do not give false testimony under oath. I hate lying, injustice, and violence (Zechariah 8:16-17).

The Christian is responsible for his own life. It must be an example of goodness. He is, as you will remember from Lesson 2, to be holy as His Father is holy. So, he should try, in so far as his position allows, to bring about right and justice in his community. If you want to

God Sent You to Care for the World

know more about how you can do this, there is another ICI course about the Christian and his community which can help you.

For You To Do

3 Circle the letter before each statement below that shows a good Christian action.
  a Told a shopkeeper he had given you too much change and returned it.
  b Told your boss that you were late to work and therefore should not receive so much pay.
  c Said that you were not the one who made a mistake when you did.
  d Suggested to your neighbors that you all collect food and clothing to help a poor widow and then keep it.
  e Found good things to say about a person nobody likes.

4 List some ways you can show your community that you care for them.

SALT FLAVORS: SPREADING THE MESSAGE OF GOD

Objective 3. *Explain how God wants to use you to tell others about Him.*

It is amazing to think that God needs *us*. Yet that is His plan. He has chosen for the good news of Jesus Christ to be told to the world by men and women—by *us*!

We who have become the children of God are the salt of the earth. Remember that salt not only preserves and purifies, it flavors. Something which salt has touched tastes salty. God's purpose is that His salt—His children—should cover the whole earth until people everywhere are made salt too.

The apostle Paul says the same thing using a different word-picture: perfume or incense. I expect you know about these. Perfume is made from sweet-smelling flowers and incense from sweet-smelling spices. When someone opens a bottle of perfume or burns an incense-stick, the fragrance spreads quickly.

Just as with salt, a little goes a long way. Soon the room or the house is filled with the fragrance. People who enter can smell it at once. They may like it; they may dislike it; but they know it's there. That is how it is with Christians, says Paul.

> God uses us to make the knowledge about Christ spread everywhere like a sweet fragrance. For we are like a sweet-smelling incense offered by Christ to God, which spreads among those who are being saved and those who are being lost (2 Corinthians 2:14-15).

There are many lessons to be learned from this passage. Notice first that it is *God's* plan to reach the world, not ours. As servants of God (as well as children) we are under orders to tell others about Jesus Christ, our Lord and Savior. Remember what Jesus said before He returned to heaven:

> Go, then, to all peoples everywhere and make them my disciples: baptize them in the name of the Father, the Son, and the Holy Spirit, and teach them to obey everything I have commanded you (Matthew 28:19-20).

The order to go and make disciples—to teach them about Christ and about Christian ethics—is followed by a wonderful promise: "I will be with you always." This underlines the idea that God *uses* us. We are not alone; we do not have to rely on our own power or wisdom. We have our faithful friend, the Holy Spirit, to help us.

This was the other promise made by Jesus, when He told His disciples about God's plan:

> But when the Holy Spirit comes upon you, you will be filled with power, and you will be witnesses for me in Jerusalem, in all of Judea and Samaria, and to the ends of the earth (Acts 1:8).

As we are continually filled with the Spirit, we become sensitive to God's leading. He uses us to speak to the people we meet. He gives us the wisdom to know how best to speak to them, according to their understanding and need. We do not have to be nervous or anxious: it is the work of the Holy Spirit, not ours, to convince people that they need Jesus as Savior (John 16:8-11).

What is our job? It is to be used by God. It is to be witnesses. Now a witness is a person who knows something by personal experience and tells about it. Jesus' disciples were witnesses to the fact that Jesus was raised from the dead (Acts 3:15). Everywhere they went, they told people that they had seen Jesus alive again. Then they explained what Jesus' resurrection meant: He was indeed the Son of God; He had died for men's sins; if men believed on Jesus, their sins would be forgiven and they would become children of God.

Your just and loving actions are a witness to the world. But they are a *silent* witness. Salt is good for preserving and purifying, but if it has no taste, it isn't really salt. Jesus said that salt without saltiness "has become worthless" (Matthew 5:13). Even our good lives are useless to God if people do not understand how they have become good. We have to *tell* people.

Peter and John healed a lame man at the Beautiful Gate of the temple (Acts 3). When the people saw what happened they were amazed. But they were not ignorant long about how the miracle had happened. Peter quickly explained: it was the power of Jesus and faith in His Name that made the man well (Acts 3:16).

Peter pointed others to Jesus and urges us to do the same.

> But have reverence for Christ in your hearts, and honor him as Lord. Be ready at all times to answer anyone who asks you to explain the hope you have in you, but do it with gentleness and respect (1 Peter 3:15-16).

Notice that our witness must be wise. It must be gentle, without harsh condemnation; it must be respectful, without false superiority. If you have not already studied the ICI course, *Personal Evangelism*, you should do so. It contains much good advice and will help you be a wise and effective witness for Jesus Christ.

Finally, when you proclaim the gospel by your witness, there will be results. Paul tells us that our fragrance will be spread "among those who are being saved and those who are being lost" (2 Corinthians 2:15). This is to reassure you that you are not responsible for making people Christians. You cannot force them into God's kingdom. You can only represent God as His ambassador. You can show and persuade. But it is each individual's choice to accept or reject the message of reconciliation.

> Here we are, then, speaking for Christ, as though God himself were making his appeal through us. We plead on Christ's behalf: let God change you from enemies into his friend! Christ was without sin, but for our sake God made him share our sin in order that in union with him we might share the righteousness of God (2 Corinthians 5:20-21).

Praise God! You are already His friend. Praise God! You are sharing His righteousness. Praise God! You are being used by God to spread His gospel. Praise God! Your new life in Christ is being put into practice in your attitudes and actions.

For You To Do

5 Circle the letter before each TRUE statement which describes a good witness.
   a I don't have to tell people about Jesus; they can just see I'm a Christian by my actions.
   b I need to have the Holy Spirit's help when witnessing.
   c I should keep on talking to a person about Jesus until he finally gives up.
   d I can tell people what Jesus has done for me and for other Christians I know.
   e Words about Jesus' life and the way I live as a Christian should not conflict.

6 Pray, asking the Holy Spirit to lead you to someone to whom you can witness. Ask His guidance in how you can best share your Savior. Pray for this person for several days before talking to him. When he accepts Jesus as his Savior, encourage him to learn more by reading his Bible and by taking an ICI course such as *Your New Life*.

Check your answers.

Now you are ready to fill out the last half of your student report for Lesson 5-8. Review these lessons, then follow the instructions in your student report. When you send your answer sheets to your instructor, ask him about another course of study.

Check Your Answers

3 a Told a shopkeeper he had given you too much change and returned it.
  b Told your boss that you were late to work and therefore should not receive so much pay.
  e Found good things to say about a person nobody likes.

1 Your answer.

4 Your answer may be different but some ways would be:
Be a friend to your neighbor.
Help the needy whenever you can.
Show them honor and love.

2 Your answer.

5 a False.
  b True.
  c False.
  d True.
  e True.

One Final Word

This is a special kind of book because it was written by people who care about you. These are happy people who have found good answers to many of the questions and problems which trouble almost everyone in the world. These happy people believe that God wants them to share with others the answers they have found. They believe that you need some important information in order to answer your own questions and problems and find the way of life that is best for you.

They have prepared this book in order to give you this information. You will find this book based on these fundamental truths:

1. You need a Savior. Read Romans 3:23, Exekiel 18:20.
2. You cannot save yourself. Read 1 Timothy 2:5, John 14:6.
3. God desires that the world should be saved. Read John 3:16-17.
4. God sent Jesus who gave his life to save all those who believe in Him. Read Galatians 4:4-5, 1 Peter 3:18.
5. The Bible shows us the way of salvation and teaches how to grow in the Christian life. Read John 15:5, John 10:10, 2 Peter 3:18.
6. You decide your eternal destiny. Read Luke 13:1-5, Matthew 10:32-33, John 3:35-36.

This book tells you how to decide your destiny, and it gives you opportunities to express your decision. Also, the book is different from others because it gives you a chance to contact people who prepared it. If you want to ask questions, or explain your needs and feelings, you may write to them.

In the back of the book you should find a card called *Decision Report and Request Card*. When you have made a decision, fill out the card and mail it as indicated. Then you will receive more help. You may use the card to ask questions, or make requests for prayer or information.

If there is no card in this copy of the book, write to your ICI instructor and you will receive a personal answer.